ART OF THE 1930s

Edward Lucie-Smith

ART OF THE 1930s

THE AGE OF ANXIETY

for Pat Warner

First published in the United States of America in
1985 by RIZZOLI INTERNATIONAL
PUBLICATIONS, INC.
597 Fifth Avenue, New York, NY 10017

**Library of Congress Cataloging in Publication
Data**

Lucie-Smith, Edward.
  Art of the 1930s.

  Bibliography: p.
  Includes index.
  1. Art, Modern—20th century—Themes,
  motives. 2. Art, Modern—20th
  century
I. Title.
N6493 1930.L8   709'.04'3   85–42813
ISBN 0–8478–0609–X

Designed by Joyce Chester
assisted by Sheila Sherwen
Index by Vicki Robinson

Printed and bound in Italy

Half title page
1. Edward Hopper
Early Morning, 1930

Oil on canvas
36 × 24in/91.4 × 61cm
Whitney Museum of American Art,
New York, (Visual Arts Library)

Title page
2. Pablo Picasso
Guernica, 1937

Oil on canvas
137½ × 306in/349.2 × 777cm
Madrid, Prado Museum (Visual
Arts Library)

Opposite
3. Barbara Hepworth
Pierced Form, 1931

Pink alabaster
10in/25.4cm high
By courtesy of the trustees of the
late Barbara Hepworth

Contents

Author's Note

It has been customary to see the history of Modernism in the visual arts as something self-contained, and to write it only with reference to the Modern Movement and its developments. This book aims to do something different. It is not a history of styles. It takes a particularly crucial epoch, and tries to relate the Modernist painting and sculpture of the period to other developments, many of them deeply hostile to everything the artists of the avant-garde stood for. This was particularly true of the neo-conservative art that developed under official patronage in Nazi Germany and in the Soviet Union. It is because the social and political context is so crucial that the chapters on the art of the dictatorships have been placed first in the book, instead of being relegated to the margin, as is usually the case.

It so happens that this arrangement makes certain other points as well. It not only demonstrates the similarities between the art of Nazi Germany and Soviet Russia, it helps to draw attention to the similarities as well as the differences between the democratic and anti-democratic art-worlds. Hitler and Stalin believed in a populist art, though they interpreted the concept to suit themselves. This was matched by a more complex populism elsewhere. Murals are among the most typical products of the 1930s – they flourished particularly in Italy, Mexico and the United States, but are also found frequently in other societies. Both Picasso and Matisse, for example, attempted important murals or mural-like paintings. These murals are symbolic of a wish to make art public and accessible again, after the hermeticism of modern art's beginnings. Many of the murals painted during the decade had political or social themes of a kind that would have been avoided during the 1920s, and this reflects an impulse towards political and social involvement that manifested itself in many other ways. I have tried to show what some of these were.

Having committed myself to a broad canvas, I have been forced to write selectively about individual artists. Some, though their importance is well-established, receive comparatively cursory treatment, because the work they did during the 1930s is not absolutely central to my view of the decade. Paul Klee is a case in point. In addition, I have sometimes illustrated a particular theme, such as urban Social Realism

in America, through the work of just one or two artists – Philip Evergood and William Gropper, rather than Ben Shahn. The reason is that Evergood and Gropper seem more closely contained within the epoch, and more typical of it. Artists are discussed, not according to some fixed hierarchy of merit, but because of the light they cast on the period as a whole.

Obviously, in making a book of this kind I have called on the help of many people. My special thanks, however, go to Celestine Dars, who has been responsible for doing the picture research, and to Caroline Zubaida, who has taken so much trouble in editing my text.

4. Diego Rivera
Mural at the Palacio Cortés,
Cuernavaca

Margaret Collier/Robert Harding
Picture Library

List of Paintings and Sculptures

reproduced in the book

Introduction

It may seem rash to claim that the painting and sculpture of the 1930s are still consistently misunderstood – more so, perhaps, than the art of any decade since 1900. It is not that the period arouses no interest. Recently there have been quite numerous studies devoted to, or at least touching upon, the art produced between 1930 and 1940 – one of the most strained, anxious and sinister periods in modern history. Max Beckmann, for example, has at last been recognized for what he is – a modern master – and the work produced during his years of exile has played an important part in this re-evaluation. Edward Hopper, largely responsible for creating our image of what America was like in the 1930s, has been the subject of an international touring exhibition. In 1982 a huge survey show was held at the Palazzo Reale in Milan, which explored what was previously almost *terra incognita* – the art, architecture and design produced in Italy during the ten years before World War II. The exhibition contradicted many of the assumptions previously held concerning art and artists under Mussolini's Fascism.

Despite this, however, there has been a twofold problem. First, a tendency to treat the art of the 1930s as being essentially a bridge between two more interesting and vital epochs. Sometimes the decade is seen as the period when the avant-garde, hitherto triumphant, suddenly found itself under siege – more intensely beleaguered than it had been even at its beginnings. This is in some respects true enough. It was not merely under siege but in some places, notably Nazi Germany and Soviet Russia, it was actually defeated. Or else the 1930s are seen as the epoch in which certain ideas germinated which were only to burst into flower in the years following 1945. This is the attitude still conventionally adopted in discussions of American art.

The other aspect of the problem is political – or rather, to be more precise, it turns on the relationship between the visual arts and politics. It has been conveniently forgotten that the political radicalism which attracted many modern artists in the years before 1914 was the radicalism of the right. Marinetti and his followers were typical examples of this, and so were the majority of the English Vorticists. It was the Russian Revolution of 1917, and the political convulsions that took place in defeated Germany immediately after World War I, that

10

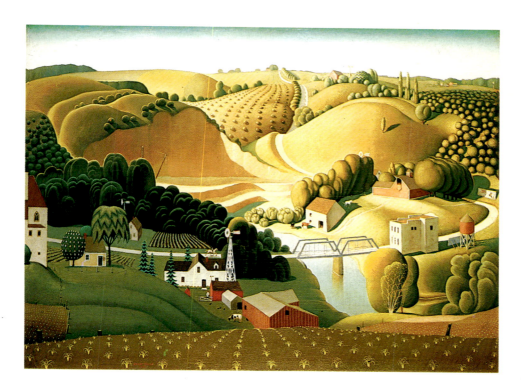

5. Grant Wood
Stone City, Iowa, 1930

Oil on wood,
$30\frac{1}{4} \times 40$in/76.8 × 101.6cm
Joslyn Art Museum

tended to cement the alliance between the avant-garde and the left. But, even from its beginnings, the relationship was an uneasy one. In Russia itself it became increasingly strained, and collapsed altogether in 1932, when the Central Committee of the All Union Communist Party officially abolished all artistic groupings of whatever kind, and took complete official control of the artistic life of the country. This was followed two years later by the formulation of the principle of Socialist Realism, defined as: 'the truthful depiction of reality in its revolutionary development,' but interpreted as a command that artists should return to the strictest kind of nineteenth-century academicism applied to subjects that glorified the regime. No other form of artistic expression was henceforth to be permitted.

In the surviving democracies, the avant-garde struggled with its own confusions. Radical artists found it difficult to give up the idea that Russia was their natural ally, especially when everything they believed in politically was being increasingly threatened by the Fascist dictatorships. But Russia, just as much as Nazi Germany, now rejected all the aesthetic principles on which they based their work. The conflict between political and other loyalties manifested itself in its most dramatic form within the Surrealist Movement, simply because this offered the most structured and doctrinaire expression of radical beliefs in the arts. What was perhaps the most memorable explosion triggered off by this conflict occurred between writers, rather than between artists. In late 1930, the poet Louis Aragon attended the Second International Congress of Revolutionary Writers in Kharkov, having made many promises to his Surrealist colleagues that he would put forward their point of view. Instead he capitulated completely to his hosts and, on his return, published a violently inflammatory poem, *Front Rouge*, calling for the killing of social democratic leaders. The French government promptly prosecuted him for incitement to murder. Aragon was duly defended by André Breton and other leading Surrealists, but in terms that implied his text was not to be taken seriously – that its incitations were in fact extravagant and irrational metaphors of a kind already associated with Surrealist doctrine. Aragon disavowed his allies, and the breach between the Surrealist Movement and official Communism was never healed, though Breton continued to make strenuous efforts to repair it, which were almost casually brushed off.

Elsewhere, however, and particularly in America, suspicious minds continued to associate avant-garde art with some form of 'bolshevism'. Experimental artists thus enjoyed a damaging reputation for being subversive without receiving much support from committed leftists, who might in other circumstances have been their natural allies.

In America, suspicion that any form of advanced art was aimed at overthrowing the existing social order was inevitably fanned by the amount of publicity accorded to a new form of art from south of the border – Mexican Muralism. This was not the creation of the 1930s. **4** Diego Rivera, the founder of the movement, had lived in Paris from 1911 to 1921. During that period he was strongly influenced by Cubism, and vestiges of the style remained with him throughout his life. In 1921 he returned to Mexico, determined to create a new form of art that would reflect the circumstances he found there. His first mural was painted in 1922, and other mural painters sprang up in his wake, notably David Alfaro Siqueiros and José Clemente Orozco. The style they evolved was a boldly effective but tempered version of figurative Modernism, containing both Cubist and Expressionist elements. The content of their work was unashamedly left wing, and both Rivera and Siqueiros were prominent members of the Communist Party. This did not prevent their extending their activities to the United States. In the 1930s all three leading muralists executed commissions there, which were frequently a focus for violent political controversy. The most publicized of these controversies was the one aroused by Rivera's murals for the RCA Building in the Rockefeller Center in New York. Begun in 1933, these were destroyed before their completion because of their unacceptable political content.

Mexican Muralism is of major importance in a number of very different ways. The aspect most often cited is the influence the Mexicans had on young artists who were to become the leaders of the New York School during the next decade. In 1935–6, for example, Siqueiros ran an Experimental Workshop in New York. He demonstrated the use of industrial paints, such as Duco, and recommended the drip technique as a way of generating images. One of the artists who attended this workshop was Jackson Pollock. To put the emphasis here is to treat the 1930s in the now customary way, as preparatory to more important developments which followed later. It is worth looking at things from another angle. Mexican Muralism is both the first major modern art movement to have based itself outside Europe, and something that shows a reversion to what Modernism had tended to downgrade. It combines the search for a strictly national identity with the desire to communicate specific, non-aesthetic content to a wide audience.

In anti-modern guise these endeavours can be found elsewhere – in the political art that was produced in Russia and in Germany. The links to Russia are close – Rivera thought of himself as producing his own version of Socialist Realism, but his art benefits both from an intractable idiosyncrasy of style and from the fact that he worked for a regime too weak to impose a strict control on what he did. In fact, one of the things that modulates his particular form of realism is the desire to be visibly Mexican – to give a voice to a culture that in his view had been repressed. A very similar nationalism can be found in the work of the American Regionalists, such as Thomas Hart Benton and Grant Wood; and it is also expressed, though more subtly, in that **5** of Hopper.

Mexican Populism is also a theme that finds many echoes elsewhere. The influence is direct in the work of Benton, but something similar

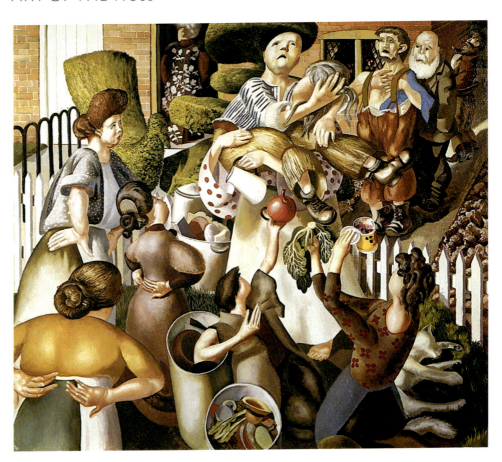

6. Stanley Spencer
The Dustmen, or the Lovers,
1935

Oil on canvas
45¼ × 45¼in/115 × 115cm
Laing Art Gallery, Newcastle Upon
Tyne

6

can also be found in what was being produced in England at the same period by Stanley Spencer and by the ex-Vorticist William Roberts. There are strong traces of the same thing to be found in Fernand Léger, though his most powerful paintings of this kind were not produced until after 1945. The Populist idiom acknowledges the existence of Modernism – it is not an attempt to put the clock back, in the Russian or German fashion. The large, simplified forms are rooted in Cubism, but it is Cubism stripped of almost everything that might puzzle or disturb the unsophisticated viewer.

It was not merely that much of the art produced in the 1930s took a Populist stance – it was also that those commissioning it often tried to link it to what they thought of as popular needs. An outstanding example was the programme of federal patronage under the American New Deal that aimed, among other things, to place murals in post offices all over the United States. These were commissioned by the Treasury Section of Painting and Sculpture, and there was a complex interaction between the essentially élitist attitudes of those running the programme and their desire to provide art that people on the spot would enjoy. The pattern of competitions and consultations that evolved was very different from the way in which modern art had been supported by its earlier patrons.

The most celebrated mural of the period, however, belongs neither to Mexico nor the United States. It is the large painting Picasso created for the Spanish Pavilion at the Paris Exposition Universelle of 1937. *Guernica* expresses horror and indignation at the bombing of the Basque capital by Spanish nationalist forces at the beginning of the Civil War – a cause that united all shades of opinion on the left. In the composition Picasso used images, such as the dying horse and the weeping woman, that he had made his own in other and more private contexts. The painting is thus a universalization of feelings that had already obsessed the artist for some years. This increases its emotional force, which is something that can be felt by everyone despite the fact that the actual pictorial language remains quite esoteric. *Guernica* is the closest the 1930s came to a genuine reconciliation between Populism and Modernism. Impulses which otherwise seem to be opposed here become equal partners.

Modernist élitism survived throughout the decade, but was subtly transformed. Thanks very largely to Diaghilev's Ballets Russes, the avant-garde arts had begun to penetrate the purely fashionable world before World War I. The process was accelerated after the Russian Revolution, when Diaghilev's company was cut off from its roots. Always very quick to seize on any aesthetic novelty, Diaghilev saw possibilities in Surrealism almost as soon as the movement was founded. In 1926 he entrusted the décor for Constant Lambert's ballet *Romeo and Juliet* to Joan Miró and Max Ernst – much against the composer's own wishes. After Diaghilev's disappearance from the scene, the Surrealist Movement, despite its commitment to the left, enjoyed increasing *réclame* in fashionable circles.

The first major Surrealist painter to defect from the political ideology approved by Breton was Salvador Dali, who was duly denounced by his former colleagues and rechristened 'Avida Dollars'. His success in the *beau monde* was enormous, and he triggered off a fashion for Surrealism in general. His imagery was popularized by

2

leading couturiers, most of all Schiaparelli, and eventually became common currency with window-dressers and advertising designers everywhere.

A high-water mark of Surrealist success was the International Surrealist Exhibition held in 1938. Its setting was the Galerie des Beaux-Arts, owned by Georges Wildenstein, the most powerful dealer in Paris. The opening was a triumph for the organizers — one journalist said wryly to Breton that he had never seen so many grand people trampled on since the disastrous fire at the Bazar de la Charité in 1897. A success of this kind did not imply universal acceptance of Surrealist doctrines, but it did show the degree to which they had penetrated the consciousness of those who were still largely responsible for creating taste. Modern art was no longer a semi-secret conspiracy in the studios of Montmartre.

Indeed one reason why art historians find the 1930s hard to bring into focus is the fact that certain major Modernists had succeeded in breaking loose from the structure of movements and -isms that had hitherto been an adequate way of describing the progress of twentieth-century art. Two cases in point are Matisse and Bonnard. Both men had turned their backs on Paris and lived in comparative isolation in the South of France. There Bonnard quietly pursued his obsession with his neurotic wife Marthe. Matisse was more in the public view — he painted a large decoration for the Barnes Foundation at Merion, Pennsylvania in 1930–3, and at the beginning of the 1930s he was the subject of no less than four major retrospective exhibitions — in Berlin, Paris, Basle and New York. These powerfully reaffirmed the artist's view of what painting was about — that it was primarily a matter of *luxe, calme et volupté*.

These exhibitions also had a less specific function. Though Matisse himself had ceased to live and work in Paris, they reaffirmed the supremacy of Paris itself. This supremacy was reinforced by the changed political climate elsewhere. In the 1920s leading Russian artists, such as Chagall, had emigrated and settled in a city that already seemed like a second home to them. Now Kandinsky, as much German as he was Russian through his connection first with the Blaue Reiter then with the Bauhaus, left Germany. He settled in Paris when the Nazis came to power in 1933 and became a French citizen in 1939. His example was followed by many others.

Less celebrated artists sometimes went further afield. Hans Hofmann, who had run his own art school in Munich between 1915 and 1930, began to teach in America in the early 1930s, and settled definitively in New York in 1934. Josef Albers, who had worked at the Bauhaus until its closure, transferred his activities to Black Mountain College in North Carolina. Both men were pedagogues of genius, and they did much to influence the direction taken by American art. Many American artists, despite the popular success of Regionalism, remained fixated by the European styles they associated with Paris, even though, in many cases, they had never visited the city. Perhaps the strangest case of all is provided by the Armenian immigrant Arshile Gorky, who in his own work seemed determined to recreate the whole development of European Modernism. Julien Levy, who was to become his dealer, told Gorky in the mid-1930s that his work was skilful but too Picassoid. 'I was *with* Cézanne for a long time,' Gorky replied, 'and now, naturally, I am *with* Picasso.' Devoted impersonation was the highest tribute he could pay.

Yet it is not merely the purely aesthetic conflicts that make the painting and sculpture of the 1930s so fascinating, even when they are as complex as those we find in the United States. What gives the art of the period its special interest is the fact that almost always it asks us to consider the relationship between the creative artist and the society he lives in. Today we see a renewed preoccupation with the relationship between art and society, art and politics. But these relationships remain profoundly uneasy, and in some aspects could also be described as unconsciously dishonest at best or hypocritical at worst. It is fascinating to see how the artists of fifty years ago faced some of the same problems – the perspective is perhaps just long enough to allow us to arrive at a fairer verdict on their successes and failures than we can on those of the present moment.

The End of Weimar and the Making of Nazi Art

The central event in the history of the visual arts during the 1930s was the National Socialist take-over in Germany, and the persecution of Modernism that followed. This was not the first set-back suffered by modern art: it was already under attack in the Soviet Union, and it was far from comfortably established in England or in the United States. But it was the most brutal, the most dramatic, and to all appearances the most complete. The Nazi attack on Modernism had far-reaching consequences still felt today, both because it brought about a diaspora of major artists that led eventually to the post-war supremacy of the United States; and because modern art and the struggle against Fascism became thoroughly identified with one another, to the huge benefit of the avant-garde when the Fascist regimes were defeated.

But the National Socialists did not merely attempt to destroy modern art – they tried to replace it with a different form of expression. Until the 1970s the art they patronized remained almost undiscussable. The first major attempt to study it seriously was made in connection with an exhibition held in Frankfurt in 1974, nearly thirty years after the downfall of the Third Reich. And even now the assumption is that the art produced by Nazism was all of the lowest quality, irremediably corrupt, and that it possesses no relationship with the other artistic phenomena of its time. For example, though the Pompidou Centre included some Nazi painting in its major survey exhibition, *Les Réalismes 1919–1939*, mounted in 1981, the exhibits in this category were carefully segregated – the implication being that they should be approached by the spectator in a totally different way from the other items in the show. The wariness shown by the organizers with regard to art of this type is understandable, and it must have taken courage to decide to include it at all. Yet to put it in quarantine, as *Les Réalismes 1919–1939* did, is to deny it quite a large part of its significance. The fact remains that the art the Nazis encouraged and patronized was not *sui generis*: it possessed not only clear historical connections, but equally obvious links with kinds of art being produced elsewhere during the same decade. It is important to see what these connections were if we are to arrive at any coherent view of the 1930s considered as a whole.

7. Oskar Martin Amorbach
The Sower, 1937

Oil on wood
$99\frac{3}{4} \times 60\frac{3}{16}$in/253.5 × 153cm
Collection of the Federal Republic
of Germany (Weimar Archive)

19

8. John Heartfield
John Heartfield with Hitler

Photomontage
(Visual Arts Library)

Before turning to what was produced under National Socialist patronage, it is necessary to describe briefly what it displaced, and to show how the Nazis set about dismantling the cultural apparatus of the Weimar Republic.

Though Weimar was a regime founded on a defeat, it was in many respects more vigorous culturally than the nations who emerged as victors from World War I. France had been the cradle of Modernism,

20

but for French artists the 1920s were largely a period of consolidation. The only important new movement was Surrealism, founded in 1924; and Surrealism owed its existence in large part to the theories of a Viennese, Sigmund Freud, fused with the nihilism of the Zürich Dadaists, themselves mostly from German or German-speaking backgrounds. It was in Germany, not in France, that the feeling took root that Modernist principles were now ready to permeate the very fabric of society. The evolution from pre-war Expressionism to the *Neue Sachlichkeit*, or New Objectivity, involved a transition from the idea of a single, unique consciousness, anguished by the struggle to make itself understood, to that of a collective consciousness, expressing the needs and thoughts of beings who were primarily social animals.

The Nazis did not politicize the German art of the period; it was already highly political. The majority of the leading artists who lived and worked in Germany during the 1920s identified themselves with the left, and often specifically with the Communist party, whom the National Socialists regarded as their chief opponents in the struggle for power. The roster of radically inclined artists' organizations began with the Novembergruppe, founded in 1918 when defeated Germany was still in chaos. Among its successors was the so-called 'Rote Gruppe', founded in 1924, specifically an organ of the KPD (the German Communist Party). Its membership was distinguished: Georg Grosz was its chairman; Rudolf Schlichter and John Heartfield were its secretaries; and in its ranks were Otto Dix and Otto Nagel. The Nazi party was given very specific reasons to dislike these men and what they produced. Heartfield's satirical photomontages, for example, constitute some of the most telling attacks made on Hitler and his henchmen in the period immediately before they achieved power.

10
9

8

The political and social involvements of the German avant-garde gave it a great deal of visibility as far as the ordinary public was concerned. But, as Hitler was shrewd enough to sense, reactions were not always positive, even among those with the same political convictions. The avant-garde might identify itself with 'the workers', but it was still suspected of being élitist. It was equated with the garish

21

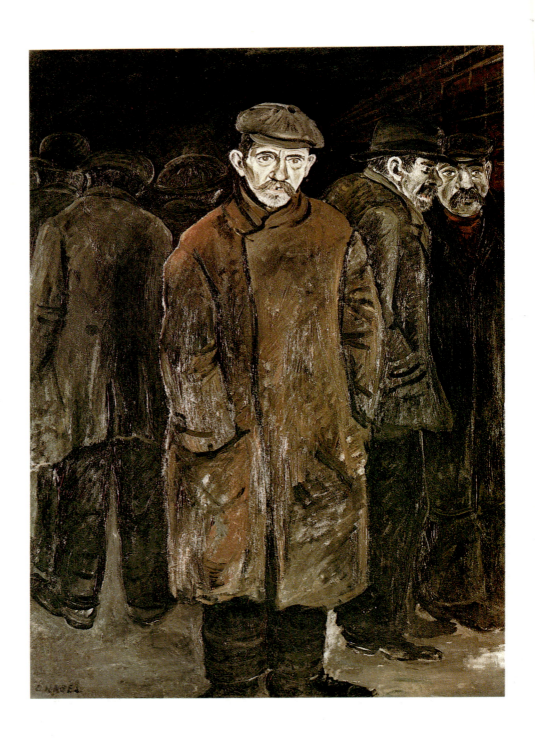

9. Otto Nagel
Workhouse Inmate, 1928

Oil on canvas
$55\frac{1}{2} \times 39\frac{5}{16}$in/141 × 100cm
National Gallerie East Berlin

new urban culture that had sprung up in Germany since 1918. Some of its most prominent patrons were *nouveaux riches* who had risen thanks to the collapse of the old social order. Its satires on post-war morals served only to identify it the more closely with modern decadence. Its stylistic and social experiments were rooted in humiliation and disaster, and even its professed internationalism could be made to seem like a deliberate insult to national pride. The Nazis hated the

22

representatives of the modern movement because of their evident hostility to National Socialism and its leaders. But they felt an even deeper and more instinctive hatred for the movement itself as something inimical to their dream of what Germany should become, and they sensed an echo of this hatred in people who were otherwise politically moderate.

The first warning about what the Nazis might do to modern art if they ever governed Germany came in 1930, and was directed at a celebrated and controversial avant-garde institution – the Bauhaus. The Bauhaus was the outcome of the merger of the Weimar Academy of Art and the School of Arts and Crafts in the same city. Under the leadership of the Modernist architect Walter Gropius, it came into being in 1919, in the immediate aftermath of Germany's defeat. Though the Bauhaus began with a heavy bias towards the crafts, this apparent traditionalism did not guarantee its innocence and it soon attracted opposition from local nationalists for what were even then described as 'Spartacist-Jewish' tendencies.

Gropius himself was certainly left wing, but only in a rather cautious way. Soon after the Bauhaus began operations he said in reply to a questionnaire: 'I am convinced that for all its evil concomitants Bolshevism is probably the only way of creating the preconditions of a new culture in the foreseeable future.' In the chaotic Germany of the period immediately after the Armistice, many people in Gropius's position felt the same. He was nevertheless opposed to the school compromising itself by open intervention in political events and on occasion restrained the left-wing enthusiasm of his students. Meanwhile the Bauhaus flourished; it abandoned its earlier Utopianism and became increasingly identified with a strictly rational attitude towards industrial design. Through its influence over German manufacturers it gave a new look to many of the accoutrements of daily life, and the products and architectural conceptions associated with it were closely linked with the new life style German progressives were trying to create.

Though its reputation flourished, its base became insecure. Weimar was situated in the state of Thuringia, which was responsible for financing the school. Thuringia, even for the Germany of the time, had a particularly stormy political climate. In 1925 Gropius, threatened with closure by a hostile state government, moved the Bauhaus to Dessau, nearer Berlin, where he successfully re-rooted it and erected a new group of buildings which attracted visitors worldwide.

In 1929 a new round of elections in Thuringia produced a large increase in the Nazi vote and as a result Wilhelm Frick was appointed state Minister of Education in January 1930: the first member of his party to hold a ministry in any state government. Significantly, one of Frick's preoccupations was to erase any lingering traces of the Bauhaus in its former home. He had paintings by Bauhaus-connected artists removed from the Weimar gallery, and whitewashed the murals by Oskar Schlemmer in the building formerly occupied by the school. Clearly he would have closed the Bauhaus itself if this had not for the moment eluded his grasp.

The Nazi triumph in 1933 brought with it an immediate campaign against art variously described as 'Bolshevist', 'Marxist', 'Jewish' and 'Degenerate'. These were catch-all labels, and anyone who tries to make a rationally ordered list of the qualities that were anathema to

11. Oskar Schlemmer
Concentric Group, 1925

38⅜ × 24⅜in/97.5 × 62cm
Staatsgalerie, Stuttgart

24

12. Walter Gropius
The workshop block and entrance of the Dessau Bauhaus

The Architectural Association, London

National Socialist theoreticians will soon realize the hopelessness of the enterprise. It is, of course, possible to see that certain categories of modern art attracted hostility even more inevitably than others. Among these were anything by an artist known to be Jewish by birth, and anything by one known to be connected with the Communist party. But it is also possible to distinguish other foci. The Nazis disliked anything that seemed to call attention to the horrors of World War I – for example, works by Grosz and Dix showing horribly crippled war veterans. They disliked satires on capitalism and pictures that showed the sleazy side of urban life, particularly its sexuality (in their view, to depict was to endorse). They were also outraged by anything that looked to them distorted, crude or unfinished – this on the whole of Expressionist art. Finally, they disliked anything that seemed hermetic – this category embraced both Cubist and entirely abstract works. In their view such works provided especially good grounds for an attack on Modernist élitism.

It is possible to identify two general theoretical ideas used by the National Socialists to justify their attack on Modernism. The first had been born at almost the same moment as Modernism itself. It stemmed from Max Nordau, whose book *Entartung* (*Degeneration*), published in 1893, was the first attempt to apply the idea of degeneration to culture (an idea rooted in the mechanistic biological science of that time). But Nordau's immediate impulse was more narrowly social and political, and was already linked to the political situation in Germany. In the late

14
13

26

13. Georg Grosz
*The Unavoidable Circle of
Crisis,* 1931–2

Pen, brush and black ink on paper
23½ × 17¾in/60 × 45cm
Christie's

nineteenth century, the German middle and lower-middle classes
were becoming increasingly disorientated by the rapid industrializa-
tion of their country, and already felt themselves to be losing their grip
on a classical culture, derived from figures like Goethe, Schiller and
Beethoven, which had hitherto united all Germans. For Nordau's
readers in the 1890s, this culture represented national identity in a
special way, since Germany's full political unification dated only from
1870. But the trauma of World War I planted the same feeling deeply in
the psyches of many of their descendants. Nordau's solution for the

27

14. Otto Dix
War, 1929–32

Triptych, oil on wood
central panel
$80\frac{5}{16} \times 80\frac{5}{16}$in/204 × 204cm
side panels $80\frac{5}{16} \times 40\frac{1}{8}$in/204 × 102cm
Predella: $23\frac{9}{16} \times 80\frac{5}{16}$in/60 × 204cm
Stäatliche Kunstsammlungen,
Dresden (Visual Arts Library)

degeneration he saw in German culture was a spiritual 'renewal' that would restore the old values, aesthetic as well as moral. Indeed, he saw an indissoluble link between the two.

Hitler himself proposed a further elaboration of Nordau's theories. He focused on the internationalism of the modern movement and its subjection to fashion, saying, in a speech made in 1937:

> Art as such is not only completely dissociated from its national origins but is also the product of a given year. This product is deemed 'modern' today and will, of course, be unmodern, that is, obsolete, tomorrow. The ultimate result of such a theory is that art and artistic activity are made equivalent to the work of our modern garment industries and fashion ateliers. In both cases, the underlying principle is to produce something different every year. First Impressionism, then Futurism, Cubism, perhaps even Dadaism, etc. ... There had been a so-called modern art in Germany until the National Socialists assumed power. This meant, as the word 'modern' implies, a different art almost every year ...

15. Max Beckmann
Portrait of Quappi with a Fox Collar, 1937

Oil on canvas
$43 \times 25\frac{1}{4}$ in/100×64 cm
Christie's

It must be admitted that this has since become a familiar argument in the mouths of all opponents of modern art (Tom Wolfe produced the most recent variation on it in his notorious tract *The Painted Word*, first published in New York in 1975).

The attack on modern art went further than mere words just as soon as the Nazis were in a position to give practical expression to their hostility. The blueprint for their assault is a five-point manifesto entitled 'What German artists expect from the New Government', published as early as March 1933. The points were as follows:

1. that all products of a cosmopolitan or Bolshevist nature will be removed from German museums and collections. First they should be brought together and shown to the public, and the public should be informed how much these works cost and which gallery officials

Wie die Verniggerung der Musik und des Theaters sollte die
Verniggerung der bildenden Kunst
den rassischen Instinkt des Volkes entwurzeln, die Grenzen des Blutes niederreißen helfen!

16. A photograph of the Exhibition of Degenerate Art held in Munich in 1937

Bilderdienst Suddeutscher Verlag, Munich

and ministers of culture were responsible for buying them. Then only one useful function remains to these works of nonart. They can serve as fuel for heating public buildings.

2. that all museum directors who sinned against a needy nation . . . by their shameless waste of public funds . . . who opened our art galleries to everything un-German . . . to be immediately 'suspended' and declared forever unfit for public office . . .

3. that from a certain date the names of artists subscribing to Marxism and Bolshevism no longer appear in print. We must abide . . . by the old law of an eye for an eye, a tooth for a tooth!

4. that in future we in this country will not have to look at apartment blocks or churches that look like greenhouses with chimneys or glass boxes on stilts, and that ways will be found to claim restitution from the criminals who grew rich perpetrating such insults against our native culture . . .

17. The Great German Art Exhibition, the exhibition of officially approved Nazi Art held in Munich in 1937

Bilderdienst Suddeutscher Verlag, Munich

5. that sculptures that are offensive to the national sensibility and yet still desecrate public squares and parks disappear as quickly as possible regardless of whether these works were created by 'geniuses' like Lehmbruck or Barlach. They must give way to the scores of artists loyal to the German tradition. The conscientious care and nurturing of all existing impulses towards a new flowering of art will have to go hand in hand with the radical negation that will free us from the nightmare of the past years! Our powers are waiting to be called to life! The people's love of art, immobilized by the *terror of artistic Bolshevism* will reawaken . . .

In November 1933 the campaign opened in earnest, when membership of the *Reichskammer der bildenden Kunste* (Reich Chamber of Visual Arts) became obligatory for all artists, as well as for a wide range of people working in art-connected professions. A central office was to decide who would be accepted, rejected, or expelled. All that was necessary for exclusion were 'indications that the person lacks the reliability or suitability necessary for the exercise of his profession'. The Nazis found numerous artists willing to accept these conditions. In 1938 the Reich Chamber of Visual Arts included 3,200 sculptors and 10,500 painters among its members.

The first phase of the war against Modernism culminated in the Exhibition of Degenerate Art staged in Munich in 1937. It is sometimes

16

forgotten that this event was conceived as one wing of a diptych. On the day before it opened, the Great German Art Exhibition, a massive display of officially approved art works, had been opened with great pomp at Munich's new Haus der Deutschen Kunst. By contrast the Exhibition of Degenerate Art occupied a few crowded rooms, where the works were arranged so as to look as insignificant and ridiculous as possible. Paintings and sculptures were accompanied and sometimes overshadowed by insulting inscriptions and captions.

One of the more notorious exhibits greeted the visitor at the very entrance to the exhibition. This was the large crucifix by Ludwig Gies, originally created as an entry for the war memorial competition at the St Marienkirche in Lübeck. Even hostile descriptions, such as this from the columns of the *Münchner neuste Nachrichten* of 20 August 1937 pay oblique tribute to its power:

> It is only a few steps to the head of the steep staircase on top of which, like a monkey on a tree, a wild phantom is crouching ... People wonder what would happen if the phantom were suddenly to jump down on them. There wouldn't be any alternative: just get your knives out! But probably he would jump down to escape as far as he could from human beings into the deepest, deepest forest, there to do what every fibre of his martyred, abused wooden body cries out for. Putrefy! putrefy! putrefy!

Gies's sculpture was chosen for its position of honour or dishonour not merely because of its actual appearance, but because of its past history. Set up soon after its completion in the ambulatory of the St Marienkirche, it aroused so much hostility that it was first vandalized, then removed as a result of a referendum. It thus became a kind of touchstone for the supporters of modern art. Carl Georg Heise, a progressive art critic who was also director of the Lübeck Museum, wrote about it thus in 1921, immediately after it had been damaged:

> It is hard to determine what is more significant: the work itself or its fate. Its existence is a tribute to the infiltration of expressionist form by a strong and particular religious emotion, and to the competent

craftsmanship of a modern sculpture in the service of a noble and timeless purpose. Its destruction, however, testifies to the increasing discrepancy between popular feeling and the artistic culture of our time – the dangerously increasing gravity of the situation we are in.

The crucifix, by far the best work of a minor artist, did not survive the Nazis, but photographs make plain its indebtedness to late-Gothic art. Certain works approved by the Nazis displayed the same influence.

In the rooms beyond Gies's sculpture could be found works by all the greatest German artists of the day, accompanied by a good number done by distinguished foreigners. The material for the exhibition came from most of the leading public galleries in Germany, the Nationalgalerie in Berlin, the Staatliche Gemälde Galerie in Dresden, the Folkwang Museum in Essen, the Städelsches Kunstinstitut in Frankfurt, and others. Among the Germans whom the public was invited to mock were Ernst Barlach, Max Beckmann, Otto Dix, Georg Grosz,

18. Adolf Wissel
Peasant Family from Kalenberg, 1939

Oil on canvas
$59\frac{1}{2} \times 78\frac{11}{16}$in/150 × 200cm
West German State Collection
(Visual Arts Library)

15

33

Erich Heckel, Ernst-Ludwig Kirchner, Käthe Kollwitz, Franz Marc, Paula Modersohn-Becker, Emil Nolde, Max Pechstein, and Karl Schmidt-Rottluff. Among the foreigners were Henri Matisse, Pablo Picasso, Jean Metzinger and Georges Rouault. A few individual inclusions aroused protest: ex-service comrades were upset because Marc had given his life for his country in World War I. Nolde, a long-time member of the National Socialist movement, penned a puzzled but vain letter of complaint to Goebbels.

As far as public attendances were concerned, the exhibition was a vast but (granted the circumstances) slightly ambiguous success. It drew just over two million visitors – until very recent times by far the largest number to have attended any exhibition of contemporary art. There were 600,000 visitors to the Great German Art Exhibition which was held simultaneously – a respectable number but less than a third of those attracted by Degenerate Art. It seems likely that, for the majority of visitors, the 1937 Exhibition of Degenerate Art constituted their first real exposure to any quantity of modern painting and sculpture. It clearly piqued their curiosity, if nothing else.

The cultural policy pursued by the Nazis evinces an almost superstitious belief in the power of art to convey both ideas and feelings. Perhaps, indeed, they believed this even more strongly than the Modernists, whom they persecuted. In the circumstances, it was unthinkable that National Socialism should be left without an art of its own. This art could not have manifested itself so quickly without the existence of an alternative tradition which long pre-dated the rise of Nazism, but which could be adapted comparatively easily to the ideological needs of the party. The art officially patronized and encouraged by the Nazis represents a partial (but not, as has been sometimes made out, a complete) reversion to conservative elements in nineteenth-century painting and sculpture. The successive Great German Art Exhibitions staged under National Socialist patronage were in many respects an attempt to revive the nineteenth-century Salons that had resisted the rise of Impressionism. Even the fashion in which the works were categorized represented a return to nineteenth-century ways of thinking. Modernism had attacked and

19. Wilhelm Leibl
Three Women in Church,
1878–81

Oil on canvas
44 × 30in/113 × 77cm
Hamburger Kunsthalle (Edimedia)

broken down the division of art into genres — still life, landscape, animal painting, figure painting (domestic or heroic), mythological painting, etc. Now this system was restored with a twofold result: a painting or sculpture once more became a manufactured item, like a table or chair, to which supposedly objective standards of workmanship could be applied. And the emphasis was placed, not on the expression of subjective emotion, but on the 'message' of the work, whether this was conveyed through narrative or allegory.

A German critic, writing for the *Deutsche Allgemeine Zeitung* of 1937 — thus at a period when the expression of opinion was already tightly controlled by the regime — compared the work on show at the Great German Art Exhibition of that year to the work of Wilhelm Leibl

20. Jules Adler
The Strike, 1899

Oil on canvas
91 × 118⅞in/231 × 302cm
Pan Museum of Fine Arts
(Visual Arts Library)

19

18

7

(1844–1900). Leibl is even now a perfectly respectable figure – the chief German disciple of Courbet, who differs from his model mainly because his paintings lack the drama and action typical of Courbet's art, and aim instead at a combination of monumental simplicity and fine technical finish. Leibl's masterpiece, his *Three Women in Church* (1878) in the Hamburg Kunsthalle, was the model for many paintings typical of the Nazi epoch – for example Adolf Wissel's *Peasant Family from Kalenberg,* painted in 1939, and chosen for exhibition in the Pompidou Centre's *Réalismes 1919–1939* exhibition of 1981. It is only when one situates Wissel's picture in its precise historical context that one sees that it does after all possess a political meaning: that it offers a helping hand to Nazi mythology about the importance of 'blood and soil'. Similarly Oskar Martin Amorbach's *The Sower,* painted in 1937, offers anyone who is aware of its context a meaning within a meaning: the seed the sower scatters is National Socialist ideas.

An appreciable proportion of Nazi-approved works were more specific than this. Sometimes the effect is unintentionally comic. Albert Otto's *The Dug Out*, painted in 1939, is a still life of the most academic kind, but the elements the artist has used are parts of a German soldier's equipment and uniform. With astonishing lack of irony, Otto has chosen to put a steel helmet where a Dutch *Vanitás* painter of the seventeenth century might have placed a skull.

The examples of Nazi art that seem the most striking today (so much so that there is a real reluctance to exhibit them under any circumstances) are those that depict the ceremonies of the regime. In academic terms, they occupy the category of 'history painting' and one direct ancestor is Jacques-Louis David's Napoleonic propaganda picture, *The Distribution of the Eagles* (1802–7). Ferdinand Staeger's *Political Front – Impressions of the Party's Day of Honour, Nuremberg, 1936* is typical in its overpowering grandiosity of style. Yet Staeger's art, and that of Paul Herrmann (another specialist in paintings of this type) is much further from nineteenth-century academic models than other works approved by the Nazis. There is an affinity, for instance, with the work of the Swiss Symbolist, Ferdinand Hodler (1853–1918).

In addition, these pictures supply an uncomfortable reminder of the perverted socialist element within National Socialism. Perhaps their closest ancestors are a group of paintings done by Socialist artists around 1900, which, like these, try to express the force of the collective will. Examples that come to mind are Jules Adler's *The Strike*, painted in 1899; and perhaps most of all Giuseppe Pellizza da **20** Volpedo's *The Fourth Estate*, painted in 1898–1901. Artists like Adler and Pellizza da Volpedo are now generally, and rightly, regarded as being among the progenitors of the Socialist Realism that also flourished in the 1930s, and perhaps even of Mexican Muralism.

But Staeger and Herrmann also have something new – a visual rhetoric that seems to derive, not from the art of the past, but from the contemporary cinema.

Though the National Socialists, when they came to power, had a broad idea of the kind of art they wanted to create, there were inevitably arguments within the party hierarchy concerning the form it should take. The most important of these arguments was between the supporters of a 'Gothic' style and a 'Classical' one. Both of these styles were deeply rooted in the German past. The first appealed to the arch-Germans and the proponents of a traditionally nationalist philosophy. It was, however, disapproved of by Hitler himself, who opted for the technocrats. He roundly condemned, in a speech made soon after he achieved power, things such as 'railroad stations in Renaissance style, street signs and typewriters with genuine Gothic letters, lyrics adapted from Walther von der Vogelweide, fashions modelled on Gretchen and Faust, paintings à la Trumpeter of Sackingen, and two-handled swords and crossbows as weapons . . .'

21 Despite the Führer's disapproval, Gothic mannerisms were not so easily suppressed. There is more than a hint of them in the designs for tapestries meant to be hung in the Reich Chancellery, which were commissioned from Werner Peiner just before the outbreak of World War II, and much publicized by the Nazi regime.

The tradition Hitler preferred was that of German classicism. The architecture of Karl Friedrich Schinkel (1787–1841), the greatest German architect of the nineteenth century, provided a model for the work of Hitler's crony Albert Speer and also for that of other architects employed by the regime. The classical manner was also used in much of the official painting and sculpture commissioned by the German government – the influences here being the paintings of artists like Christian Gottlieb Schick (1776–1812), and the sculpture of Gottfried Schadow (1764–1850). The classical style simultaneously spoke of reverence for the German past, and of imperial ambitions for the future. Hitler's own favourite artist was the classical painter Adolf Ziegler, nicknamed 'the master of German pubic hair', and, in his time away from the studio, one of the chief sniffers-out of 'degenerate art' in German institutions.

The most significant of the neo-classicists patronized by the Nazis was, however, the sculptor Arno Breker. One reason for his significance is that he is uncharacteristic of many of the things one is taught to believe about Nazi art. To demonstrate this fully, it is necessary to recount his career in some detail.

Born in 1900, Breker was the son of a sculptor, and received a conventional academic training, first in his father's studio, and later at the Düsseldorf Academy. He became aware of Modernist developments very early. In the first years of the 1920s, he was already making abstract sculptures and, even when he turned decisively towards figuration, he remained in close touch with the modernist avant-garde, visiting Paul Klee and Walter Gropius at the Weimar Bauhaus, and making a portrait head of Otto Dix.

In 1924 Breker left for Paris, where he soon built up a very wide circle of friends. Among them were Jean Cocteau; the film-director Jean Renoir; the painters Maurice de Vlaminck, André Dunoyer de Segonzac and Jean Fautrier; and fellow-sculptors as different from one another as Alexander Calder, Isamu Noguchi, Constantin Brancusi and Charles Despiau. He formed a close relationship, which amounted to discipleship, with Aristide Maillol that lasted unbroken until the latter's death in 1944. In addition to all this he attracted the attention of the powerful art dealer Alfred Flechtheim, who began to promote his work back home in Germany. By 1930 Breker was already well known and highly successful in his native country, though he continued to live and work in France.

His return home in 1934, just after the Nazis gained power, took place under the auspices of Max Liebermann (1847–1935), one of the

21. Werner Peiner
The Siege of Marienburg

Tapestry design for the Reichs
Chancellery
Bilderdienst Süddeutschen Verlag,
Munich

39

most eminent artists in Germany, and also, like Flechtheim, a Jew. Breker made a portrait of Liebermann just before the latter's death, which was probably hastened by political events, and also a death-mask at the request of the painter's widow.

Despite his associations with both the Jewish community and the avant-garde, Breker almost immediately found favour with the Nazis. In 1936 he won a silver medal in a competition held in conjunction with the Berlin Olympics of that year, and in 1938 he was commissioned to create two frowning male nudes, one brandishing a torch and the other a sword, for the entrance of the new Reich Chancellery – these were seen by his patrons as striking embodiments of their fantasies about Aryanism. During the war, Breker became an important figure in Nazi cultural diplomacy. He was given a one-man show at the Orangerie in Occupied Paris which was attended by 80,000 visitors. Cocteau, Despiau, Maillol and Segonzac were contributors to a monograph on his work, published to mark the occasion. Breker later acted as an intermediary in persuading a party of leading French artists to make a visit to Berlin. Among them was André Derain, whose reputation, so high between the wars, never recovered from this act of collaboration.

Though much of Breker's sculpture for his Nazi patrons was destroyed during the war, he was able to continue a successful career after 1945. His classical male nudes were still in demand, and he was much employed as a portraitist. His sitters included some of the leading politicians of post-war Germany, among them Ludwig Erhard; and also the leaders of various African nations, such as Sadat of Egypt, Senghor of the Ivory Coast, and Félix Houphouet-Boigny. There were also international celebrities such as Salvador Dali and the still-faithful Cocteau. Breker's bust of Cocteau, made just before the writer's death in 1963, now serves as a memorial in the chapel at Milly-la-Forêt.

Arno Breker (still alive as these words are written) ranks in the personal sense as a great survivor. But there are reasons other than purely biographical ones for paying close attention to his work. He is not a first-rate sculptor, but he does fit into a part of the twentieth-century tradition that has nothing integral to do with National

22

22. Arno Brecker
Man with a Sword, 1938

One of the statues standing in front of the new Reich Chancellery in Berlin
(Edimedia)

Socialism. Throughout Europe, during the 1920s and 1930s, there were persistent revivals of neo-classicism. These took place in both the democracies and the dictatorships – in France, their pedigree is particularly complicated. One part of the tradition, a purely sculptural one, can be traced to Rodin. Both Maillol and Maillol's exact contemporary Émile-Antoine Bourdelle reacted against Rodin's naturalism. They were influenced by the scholarly reinvestigation of Greek art then taking place which resulted in a renewed appreciation of Archaic and Early Classical styles. One of the earliest manifestations of this shift in taste is Bourdelle's *Herakles Archer*, first exhibited in

23. Emile-Antoine Bourdelle
Herakles Archer, c. 1910

Bronze
23½in/60cm high
Christie's

23 1910. *Herakles Archer* also shows evidence of the Nietzschean worship of masculine strength and force so prevalent at the period when it was created. It is perhaps the closest direct ancestor of Breker's male nudes for the Reich Chancellery. In general, Breker's sculpture is often marked by slightly mannered touches that relate it unmistakably to the Art Deco style of the sculptor's period of apprenticeship in Paris.

There is also a looser, but still recognizable link with the neo-classical style favoured by Picasso during the early 1920s, and with the manner Picasso later adopted for the etchings of the Vollard Suite, many of which depict a sculptor's studio.

Any attempt to detach Breker from the mainstream of twentieth-century art is thus doomed to failure. He was not a purely National Socialist artist, any more than he was an entirely 'academic' one, working mechanically in a dead tradition. In fact, he represented an adaptation of things that already existed within Modernism to new conditions – and in this he was not exceptional among the artists of Hitler's Germany. There is a paradox to be found here: the art most closely geared to the intimate preoccupations of the regime tended in general to be more 'modernistic' in style than that which just took care not to transgress against the new rules. The explanation is simple: the Nazis rejected and persecuted the art they perceived as modern, but their own art was nevertheless bound to innovate, as there was no art of the pre-modern epoch that addressed itself to a mass consciousness in precisely the way the party required. Yet if the Nazis saw art as a major means of communication with the mass this viewpoint was not peculiar to them: they shared it with official patrons elsewhere, who for the first time since the Middle Ages consciously thought of art as something that must and should address itself to everyone. In the 1930s art increasingly entered the public arena. We can see the results almost worldwide – in the Socialist Realist work that had become the norm in Russia; in the continuing campaign of the Mexican Muralists, and in the mural paintings of the artists employed by the Works Project Administration (WPA) in America. In all these cases, as in Nazi Germany, a new populism was linked to a resurgence of nationalism. Even where there was no direct official intervention, artists became concerned with public issues – France and Britain are cases in point. In the 1930s, though the gap of political belief was often wide, the stylistic differences between those who belonged to different creeds were not always as huge as they liked to make out, nor as we would now like to convince ourselves.

Socialist Realism in Russia

The Russian avant-garde, of the period that immediately preceded and followed the October Revolution, now attracts immense interest in the West, and has been the subject of a number of recent exhibitions. Russian Socialist Realism, on the other hand, is scarcely known in any detail outside Russia; and there are signs that even the Soviet government now regards it as being something chiefly designed for home consumption. The kind of information we have concerning it is much less detailed than what we know about the official art favoured by National Socialism (which in some respects it resembles), even though its span of existence has been much longer. In addition to this, western critics see Russian Socialist Realism almost entirely in terms of what it supplanted.

The final phase of Russian Constructivism, the avant-garde movement which had triumphed over all the others during the immediately post-revolutionary period, was 'production art'. The new phase in Constructivism's development was initiated by an exhibition held in Moscow in 1921. Entitled '5 × 5 = 25' it contained works by Alexander **24** Rodchenko, Alexandra Exter, Liubov Popova, Varvara Stepanova and Alexander Vesnin. They denounced art for art's sake and rejected studio art in favour of industrial design. In October 1922, Boris Arvatov, one of the main promoters of what came to be called Productivism, wrote as follows:

> Constructivism is socially utilitarian. Its application is situated either in industrial production (engineer-constructor) or in propaganda (constructor-designer of posters, logos, etc.). Constructivism is revolutionary not only in words but in acts. It is revolutionary by the very orientation of its artistic methods.

From this period onwards, the art of the Russian avant-garde consisted of fewer paintings and sculptures, and many more projects – generally unfinished – linked to industrial design, architecture, book design, photography, theatre and film. Film, in particular, absorbed much avant-garde energy, since it was regarded as the ultimate popular art-form, and the one that could deal most directly with the political, social and aesthetic issues of the day.

24. Liubov Popova
Composition, 1924

Oil on canvas
Galerie Jean Chauvelin, Paris
(Visual Arts Library)

25. Boris Kustodiev
Festival in Uritsky Square in Honour of the Second Comintern Congress, 1920

Oil on canvas
(Novosti Press Agency)

It was inevitable that this concentration on non-traditional formats and non-traditional uses for art should provoke a reaction – one that was supported by the leaders of the Communist party, who did not always feel comfortable with their avant-garde allies. The year of Arvatov's pronouncement, 1922, also saw the foundation of the Association of Artists of the Revolution. Its slogan was 'art to the masses', and they interpreted this phrase in a way very different from that in which the Productivists might have construed it. Figurative art with a didactic or propagandistic purpose was already coming back into fashion. Typical are Boris Kustodiev's panoramic *Festival in Uritsky Square in Honour of the Second Comintern Congress*, painted in 1920; and Yefim Cheptsov's *Meeting of a Village Party Cell*, painted in 1924. Both are forerunners of the typical Soviet art of the 1930s, and both show an obvious debt to the work of the nineteenth-century *Peredvizhniki* or Wanderers, who provide Socialist Realism with a specifically Russian source.

The Wanderers took their name from the series of touring exhibitions they organized, from the 1870s onwards – the official name of their group was the Society of Travelling Art Exhibitions. It was formed in order to express growing opposition to the academic art of the period – less its technical procedures than its élitism and estrangement from national life. Like Wilhelm Leibl in Germany, the Wanderers belonged to the current of nineteenth-century Realism –

25
26

46

they, too, can be regarded as disciples of Courbet. But their Realism took on a Russian and (in common with the literature of the period) specifically political guise, thanks to the absence of more direct means of expression under the tsarist autocracy. A feeling of kinship with the great Russian writers was expressed through superb portraits, such as Vasily Perov's of Dostoevsky (1872) and Ivan Kramskoy's of Tolstoy (painted in 1873 just as the latter was writing *Anna Karenina*). Another aspect of the Wanderers appears in incidents from Russian history, painted as an affirmation of national feeling. One of the most famous of these within Russia itself is Vasily Surikov's dramatic canvas, *The Boyarina Morosova* (1887). This shows one of the most prominent of the Old Believers (a sect that split the Russian Orthodox church in the seventeenth century) defiantly addressing a crowd as she lies in chains on a sleigh. The painting can be read as an allegory – a nationalist challenge flung down in the face of increasing westernization.

26. Yefim Cheptsov
A Meeting of a Village Party Cell, 1924

Oil on canvas
$23\frac{1}{16} \times 30\frac{1}{8}$in/58.6 × 76.5cm
Tretyakov Gallery, Moscow
(Novosti Press Agency)

28

7

There were also scenes from contemporary Russian life, often laden with explosive meaning. The most memorable are the works of the greatest of the Wanderers, Ilya Repin (1844–1930). His allusions to tsarist oppression are often specific, as in *They Did Not Expect Him* (1884), which shows a newly liberated political exile returning unannounced to his family home. *They Did Not Expect Him* is a superb piece of narrative exposition, with the reactions of the various personages carefully differentiated – the wife numbed by emotion, the young son bursting with joy, the little girl frightened because she does not recognize a father whom she hardly remembers. These paintings made a deep impression on the Russian public, and their impeccably 'revolutionary' content made it difficult for the avant-garde of half a century later to condemn them out of hand.

29

Anatoly Lunacharsky, the People's Commissar in charge of the arts, functioned to some extent as a protector of the experimentalists, but it was also he who came up with the slogan 'back to the Wanderers' when the Party decided that the new art was not functioning efficiently in a political sense. The demand that art should be 'socially utilitarian' rebounded on the Constructivists' own heads. Lenin's own tastes in the visual arts were in any case conservative, as is revealed in a conversation with Clara Zetkin, one of the founders of the German Communist Party.

> We are too great 'iconoclasts in painting' [Lenin told her]. The beautiful must be preserved, taken as an example, as the point of departure even if it is 'old'. Why turn our backs on what is truly beautiful, abandon it as the point of departure solely because it is 'old'? Why worship the new as a god compelling submission simply because it is 'new'? Nonsense! Bosh and nonsense! Here much is pure hypocrisy and of course unconscious deference to the art fashions ruling the West. We are good revolutionaries but somehow we feel obliged to prove that we are also 'up to the mark' in modern culture. I however make bold to declare myself a barbarian.

There is more than an echo here of Hitler's denunciation of modern art as mere fashionmongering, and a strong appeal to national feeling.

27. Ivan Kramskoi
Portrait of Tolstoy, 1873

Oil on canvas
(Journeyman Press)

49

28. Vassily Surikov
The Boyarina Morosova,
1884–7

Oil on canvas
Tretyakov Gallery, Moscow

30

31

In 1925 OST, the Association of Easel Painters, was founded as a riposte to the Constructivist view that easel painting no longer had any relevance. It held a series of four exhibitions between 1925 and 1928. The style typical of the artists who belonged to OST represents a transition to the fully developed Socialist Realism of the 1930s, and the group's period of activity coincides with the struggle between Trotsky and Stalin for control of the Party. Typical products of the time are Alexander Deineka's *Defence of Petrograd*, still one of the best-known of all Soviet paintings, which dates from 1927, and D. P. Shternberg's *The Agitator*, also painted in 1927.

Usually these works are described as being in some way 'expressionist', since they incorporate a certain degree of distortion. The resemblance to classic German Expressionism is, nevertheless, not particularly close. This is, rather, an oratorical style, which uses drastic simplifications and a comparatively small measure of distortion to make its points. The treatment of space in compositions by artists connected with OST may have been influenced by Soviet photography, which was then in an especially creative phase. There is a likeness to experiments then being made by Alexander Rodchenko, a leading Constructivist who had virtually abandoned painting in favour of the camera. One thing he and the OST painters have in common is the deliberate 'alienation' of the spectator. Various formal devices are used to distance the viewer from the subject and even to impose a

50

29. Ilya Repin
They Did Not Expect Him,
1884

Oil on canvas
$63\frac{3}{16} \times 66$in/160.5 $\times$ 167.5cm
Tretyakov Gallery, Moscow

30. Alexander Deineka
Defence of Petrograd, 1927

Oil on canvas
(Novosti Press Agency)

slight disorientation, so that objects or actions which might seem unremarkable in real life, are given a frisson of their own.

The decline of the Soviet avant-garde, and its confusion about the nature of its own activity and the way in which this was to be organically linked to the new Soviet society were matched by the bureaucracy's own increasing aesthetic conservatism and terror of displeasing a ruthless leadership. The late 1920s were the epoch of the controversy about 'formalism'. The term originated in the assertion made by the Constructivists that 'a new form gives rise to a new content, since form and being determine consciousness and not vice-versa.' But it soon became a catch-all word of abuse for all artistic styles that attracted the disapproval of the Soviet authorities. The Party gradually tightened its grip on what artists were doing, and the tendency culminated in a resolution of the Central Committee of the All-Union Communist Party passed in April 1932. This created the situation that still exists in Russia today. The Union of Soviet Artists was set up as a means of artistic control. Membership of it was now essential to any painter or sculptor who wished to make a career in the Soviet Union. From an organizational point of view the situation was thus closely parallel to the one created a year later in Germany, when membership of the Reich Chamber for the Visual Arts became essential to any artist who wished to pursue a professional career. In 1934 the principle of Socialist Realism – summarized with dangerous vagueness as 'the truthful depiction of reality in its revolutionary development' – was officially imposed on Soviet artists as the aesthetic norm.

The recent re-examination of National Socialist art, most of it undertaken by Marxist critics, has brought with it a strenuous effort to differentiate the art favoured by the Nazi hierarchy from the superficially similar variety that flourished at the same period in the Soviet Union. It is alleged, for example, that German artists, working for a regime that was *petit bourgeois* and nostalgic, preferred to show industrial labour as something impersonal and ant-like, whereas in Russia it is depicted as dignified and heroic. The distinction is difficult to make in practice, as examples of both modes are found in each of the two countries. Sometimes the quibbling is plainly absurd. Professor Berthold Hinz, author of the most authoritative book on National Socialist art, remarks that the panoramic quarry scenes that form a distinctive sub-genre in Nazi landscape painting seem to have been intended as 'a deterrent and a warning', because the quarrying was done by slave-labour under barbarous conditions. Here one cannot help recalling that in 1932 Rodchenko published a series of remarkable photographs of the building of the White Sea Canal. 'Constructed by prisoners, the canal was regarded by many as a testing ground not only for the strength of Soviet technology, but also for the re-education of the antisocial individual into a useful member of the collective.'*

In fact, there are both similarities and differences between the Russian and German official art of the 1930s, and both are important. The chief similarity – important because it tells us a great deal about how these paintings and sculptures were intended to affect their audience – was their mutual return to the system of genres elaborated in the nineteenth century. This tended to redirect the spectator's attention away from the style of the work, its function as a vehicle for individual expression, towards its content, which tends to have a collective rather than a personal meaning.

The main difference is one not usually cited, because it has nothing to do with choice of subject-matter or specific tricks of style. It is, rather, a question of tradition and the attitude towards it. The German return to Leibl seems debilitated – the paintings are half-hearted pastiches. The Russians recreate the nineteenth century far more convincingly. They were closer to it, and they felt more confidence in going back to the Wanderers in particular, who represented a tradition of vital political art.

The official Soviet attitude towards the function of art still remains so different from any prevailing in the West that it is worth quoting a useful reminder – a pronouncement made by a leading contemporary

* John E. Bowllt, 'Alexander Rodchenko as Photographer', in *The Avant-garde in Russia*, catalogue of an exhibition held at the Los Angeles County Museum, 8 July–29 September 1980, p. 57.

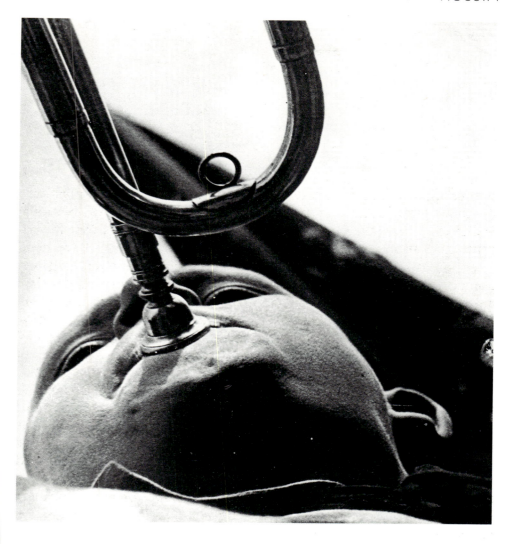

31. Alexander Rodchenko
Untitled photograph, 1930
Professor Lubomir Linhart,
Prague

Russian art-critic, Vladislav Zimenko, editor-in-chief of the art-magazine *Iskusstvo*:

Great art is not created in divorce from reality. It never breaks with the soil of life. *It imbibes the thoughts, feelings, views, concepts and dreams of the people; it is the crossroads, the focus of the ideological, moral and aesthetic currents which compound social life.*

The italics are mine. To a Russian, the emphasis would not be necessary.

Certain categories of subject-matter seem especially typical of the Soviet art of the period under discussion, though Socialist Realism has remained the officially approved Soviet style right up to the present moment. As one would expect, there are numerous posthumous portraits of Lenin, intended to stress his position as an all-wise

32. Nikolai Andreevich Andreev
Bust of Lenin 1924–9

Bronze
19¼ × 17 11/16 × 17 5/16 in/49 × 45 × 44cm
Tretyakov Gallery, Moscow (Visual Arts Library)

33

demigod. What is perhaps the most famous of all these portraits dates from 1930, though it is apparently based on studies made by the artist during Lenin's lifetime: Isaak Brodsky's *Lenin in the Smolny Institute*. The picture was so immediately successful that the artist produced some thirty replicas in the course of his career. (The widespread practice of painting replicas, and of producing co-operative works which are the product of several hands, tells us a great deal about the Socialist Realist aesthetic).

Brodsky's tersely realistic, almost photographic, image is clearly based on the example of Repin, though it is much cooler and drier in style. In a broader sense, it owes even more to J.L.David, the true inventor of political art of this type and its most successful practitioner. The image of Lenin quietly at work in the incongruous surroundings of a commandeered girls' school (which became the Bolshevik headquarters in Petrograd during the October Revolution) recalls in particular J.L.David's portrait of *Napoleon in His Study* (1812), commissioned by the Emperor's Scottish admirer the Duke of Hamilton. Though David's painting is more formal, the intention is the same: a solitary and dedicated leader is shown working for the benefit

of his people. One can apply to Brodsky's painting the art historian Dr Anita Brookner's perceptive comment about David: 'for all its hermetic and protected quality, the main feeling imparted by the image is one of human fragility.'

Equally characteristic of the period in Russia are narrative paintings that glorify the Revolution without referring to specific individuals. A painting that enjoys almost the same degree of fame in the Soviet Union as Brodsky's portrait of Lenin is Boris Ioganson's *Interrogation of the Communists*, painted in 1933. The artist himself has left an account of the genesis of this composition – it shows the frame of mind in which a successful Socialist Realist painter might set to work:

In the twenties I was working in a small theatre both as actor and artist. We put on a play from the days of the Civil War, the name of which I do not at present recall. At the headquarters of the Whites an officer with a riding crop in his hand interrogates a young communist girl. This scene, looming up in my memory . . . helped my thoughts to crystallize and prompted me to paint *Interrogation of the Communists* . . .

33. Isaac Brodsky
Lenin in the Smolny Institute,
1930

Oil on canvas
$74\frac{3}{4} \times 112\frac{15}{16}$in/$190 \times 287$cm
Tretyatov Gallery, Moscow
(Journeyman Press)

34

34. Boris Ioganson
The Interrogation of the Communists, 1933

Oil on canvas
$83\frac{1}{4} \times 109\frac{13}{16}$in/211 × 279cm
Tretyakov Gallery, Moscow
(Novosti Press Agency)

What should be the central idea of the canvas? The Bolsheviks in captivity of course. They know that the enemy will not spare them, but still they face death as victors. They stand shoulder to shoulder, their faces manly and calm, imbued with the strength to rise above their personal fates by their awareness of the justice of the Revolution. The White Guards by contrast are cold and calculating, cynical and cruel. They are motivated by low, self-centred interests, want only to order men about, live off their labour and get revenge for the privileges taken away from them. But at the same time they remain alienated from each other, each one of them an individualist, putting his own interests above everything else.

There was one detail of this composition that I wanted to emphasize: to get it across I adopted the so-called 'high eye-level'. This way I achieved the impression of a sloping floor. It looks as if the White Guards are rolling downhill while the Bolsheviks stand on the summit.

35. Alexander Deineka
Pilots of the Future, 1938

Oil on canvas
$51\frac{9}{16} \times 63\frac{3}{8}$in/131 $\times$ 161cm
Central Museum of the Armed
Forces of the USSR

Now that the conception had finally matured, had really begun to get somewhere, I had to start thinking of the details. First I changed daylight to evening, artificial light, falling directly from above on the faces of the Bolsheviks – I didn't want the onlooker to miss a single one of their features. But the depths of the room stay in half-darkness, so that the figure of the escort becomes a secondary detail and stops attracting attention. The picture thus achieves a dramatically intense character.

This account suggests how far Ioganson had succeeded in re-connecting himself with the pre-modern tradition. Certain phrases even suggest the approach that would have been taken by a Baroque religious painter called upon to depict Christian martyrs face-to-face with their persecutors. But the real link is with a kind of art that came into fashion in the late-eighteenth century and persisted into the nineteenth, that is based on an intimate knowledge of the theatre and of theatrical convention. J. B. Greuze's *The Punished Son* in the Louvre stands at the beginning of this development, and Repin's *They Did Not Expect Him* towards the end of it. Ioganson's painting is a masterpiece but (as he himself implies) a masterpiece of adroit stage-management. Even the high viewpoint and sloping floor the artist mentions suggest the theatre – we seem to be looking down at figures standing on a raked stage from a vantage point somewhere in the dress circle.

Socialist Realist painters were, of course, interested in the idea of modernity – but it is modernity narrowly interpreted as something entirely bound up with material progress. Alexander Deineka gave up the mannerisms of the OST group and succeeded in adjusting his style to the new, officially approved vision. A typical work of the period is **35** *Pilots of the Future*, painted in 1938. It shows three small boys admiring a distant seaplane. The title, and one's own knowledge of the context, enable one to decode its ideological significance. Seen through different spectacles *Pilots of the Future* might make a less specific impression. Mood and atmosphere, colour scheme and handling, all suggest a comparison to the seascapes the American realist Edward Hopper was producing at the same period.

Less happy in its effect is a painting by another former member of **36** OST, Yuri Pimenov. The painting is entitled *New Moscow* (1937), and stylistically it is a strange mixture, combining things borrowed from the cinema with a kind of much-diluted Impressionism. The spectator is apparently placed in the back seat of an open touring car which is being driven by a young woman in a modish summer dress. The broad boulevard swarms with other automobiles, and in the distance there rises the shimmering bulk of an immense construction whose size and newness are emphasized by older, lower buildings to the right and left. The picture provides a strangely dream-like and fictional vision of a city on the eve of Stalin's most savage purges.

Socialist Realism did not make the Revolution, or technological progress, its exclusive themes. In the 1930s the Russian realists looked back to the old Russia the Revolution had destroyed. Some of these recreations are as much nostalgic as they are critical. This is especially the case in the work of Pavel Korin, who at this period made a series of powerful studies for a never-completed major composition he intended to call *Vanishing Russia. Requiem*. The subject fitted the artist's own background – he had been born in the village of Palekh, where the main industry was the production of icons, and had himself trained as a traditional icon painter. Korin's backward-looking art might perhaps have brought him into disfavour – but for the fact that it happened to catch the eye of Maxim Gorky. Visiting Korin's studio in 1931, Gorky

described the study of an old nun, now in the Tretyakov, as 'genuine, wholesome, truly national art'. The choice of adjectives was every-thing an ambitious Soviet artist could have desired. Under Gorky's protection, Korin was able to travel to Italy, and used the opportunity to paint a portrait of his patron, in 1932, that stands comparison with those made by the Wanderers of the great Russian writers of an earlier generation.

Korin's art is self-evidently genuine within the terms the painter set himself, even though it represents a major anomaly in the story of twentieth-century art as this is told in most textbooks. *The Old Nun* (1930) was not intended to be complete in itself, but like many surviving Constructivist designs, was a stepping stone towards something much more ambitious. In this sense a direct comparison is

36. Yuri Pimenov
New Moscow, 1937

Oil on canvas
$55\frac{1}{16} \times 66\frac{15}{16}$in/140 × 170cm
Tretyakov Gallery, Moscow
(Novosti Press Agency)

possible, and it is not to Constructivism's advantage. *The Old Nun* has an emotional commitment, a sense of conviction that the Constructivist projects of the 1920s do not convey.

This tells one something about another, and most important difference between Socialist Realism and the art favoured by the Nazis – which is that they were born in contrasting circumstances. Whereas the avant-garde in Germany was full of vigour at the time when it was forcibly suppressed, the Russian avant-garde to some extent acquiesced in its own downfall. Its energy had already been drained by the emigration during the earlier part of the 1920s of many leading figures, worn out by the factionalism between the different movements of the time. The émigrés included Marc Chagall, Naum Gabo and Antoine Pevsner. Wassily Kandinsky returned to the West in 1921, after living in his native Russia during the war. The self-confidence of the surviving Constructivist rump (for this is what it now amounted to) was further undermined by growing doubts about whether there was in fact any role for the fine artist in Soviet society. Productivism was an explicit manifestation of these doubts. By the crucial year 1932 many of the leading avant-gardists who remained in Russia had become preoccupied with enterprises very much on the margin of fine art – Rodchenko with photography, Tatlin with his project for a man-propelled aircraft to be called the Letatlin, others with theatre design. Alexander Rodchenko, Vladimir Tatlin and even Kasimir Malevich (before his death in 1935) all produced some figurative painting in the 1930s. This seems to have been done in response to their own feelings about a changed artistic climate rather than to any direct official pressure. It won them no attention – very suddenly they had become men of the past rather than of the future.

Because Socialist Realism has long been symbolic of aspects of Soviet cultural policy that are condemned in the West, there is a reluctance to recognize that it does offer a wider range of quality than the art of National Socialism, and that its best efforts offer much more of a challenge to modernist complacency. Its worst fault is forced optimism – where the Wanderers spoke for the Opposition, this is the voice of a party in power. Typical examples are Vera Mukhina's sculpture of *A*

37

37. Kasimir Malevich
The Inhabitant of the Dacha,
1910–30

(Visual Arts Library)

Worker and Collective Farmer (1936), striding towards the future with **38**
hammer and sickle raised triumphantly aloft, and Serafina Riangina's
Higher! Ever Higher! (1934), a painting that shows a male and a female
engineer, both equally strapping, scrambling joyfully up an electric
pylon. In works such as these, the falsity of content seems to corrupt
the technical skills of the artists who have perpetrated them —
everything becomes loose, bloated and approximate.

Yet even these lapses should not prevent us from recognizing that
Socialist Realism has a profound organic connection with Russian
culture, and has been to some extent a thing of natural growth.

Paradoxically this rootedness in a particular cultural situation was
the thing that gave Socialist Realism enough force to make an impact
outside Russia, even with people who were not communist sympa-
thizers. It had a more widespread impact on the art of the 1930s than is
generally admitted today. The National Socialists were a challenge to
Modernism, and a threat to its development. They provided Modernists living in the democracies with that useful thing, an avowed and
clearly visible enemy, and the art produced under their aegis was
easily discounted. For many artists living outside Russia, especially
those with left-wing convictions, Soviet Socialist Realism was a
worrying aberration. It offered reinforcement to realist tendencies
emerging independently elsewhere, and made its influence felt even in
countries such as the United States, where the vast majority were
implacably hostile to the Soviet political system.

38. Vera Mukhina
*A Worker and Collective
Farmer*, 1936

Sculpture erected at the main
entrance to the USSR Economic
Achievement Exhibition in
Moscow
Stainless steel
Height c. 80ft/24.4m
(Novosti Press Agency)

Italy: Pluralism under a Dictatorship

It has been commonly assumed, especially outside Italy, that the art produced there under Fascism closely resembled the art produced in Germany after the Nazi triumph in 1933. This is by no means the case. Both Hitler and Mussolini were interested in art – Hitler because he was a failed painter (at one period during the 1920s he earned a poorish living from his work), Mussolini because he made his political début in a milieu where art and politics were almost inextricably intertwined. At one period Filippo Tommaso Marinetti, the founder of Futurism, had actually seen himself as Mussolini's rival.

By 1930, Mussolini had been in power for eight years. In his own estimation, he was a sophisticated and enlightened patron, who took a close interest in developments on the contemporary scene. The group most favoured by him, and by the regime in general, was the Novecento, originally founded in Milan in the same year as Mussolini's March on Rome. At this time, the membership consisted of Achille Funi, Anselmo Bucci, Piero Marussig, Ubaldo Oppi, Leonardo Dudreville, and (best-known among the group) Mario Sironi. The Novecento had their first meeting at the Galleria Pesaro in Milan the following year, and Mussolini himself was present to address them. In 1924, the group was featured at the Venice Biennale. And in 1926, on the occasion of an exhibition at the Permanente in Milan, it was enlarged and transformed into the Novecento Italiano. Among those who now **40** joined it were Massimo Campigli and Carlo Carrà. Carrà was a significant recruit because he had passed through the experience of Futurism, and had then become Giorgio de Chirico's colleague and rival in the short-lived experiment of *pittura metafisica*. He thus represented an element of continuity with the avant-garde of the prewar and war years.

The Novecento's origins were both national and international. From a purely Italian point of view it represented a rejection of the more feverish experiments made on the eve of World War I. It also reflected the nationalism of Mussolini's regime – its chief apologist, the critic Margharita Sarfatti, proclaimed that 'The word Novecento shall resound through the world again as gloriously Italian as the Quattrocento'. It aligned itself mainly through its return to sources in classical

39. Benito Mussolini, Italy's 'man of destiny', dominating the ancient city of Rome

art, especially in Roman sculpture and wall-painting, with Mussolini's bombastic ambition to create a new Roman Empire. But it also had clear links with what was going on elsewhere in Europe. France witnessed a strong classical revival at just about the same time as the Novecento was founded – its most conspicuous products were the neo-classical paintings Picasso produced during the early 1920s.

A number of Novecento artists became involved in one of the characteristic activities of the period, as popular in Italy as it was in Mexico or the United States: the painting of murals. This reached its peak during the 1930s, even though the Novecento itself had begun to be challenged by rival groups. The declared policy of Mussolini's government, to put art at the service of the people, was completely in step with the artist's own feelings. In their *Manifesto of Mural Painting*, published in December 1933, Sironi, Carrà, Campigli and Funi declared roundly that: 'art must have a social function'. These sentiments were put into effect with large-scale decorative paintings for the ambitious exhibitions typical of the time – for example, the exhibition to celebrate the tenth anniversary of Fascism staged in Rome in 1932 and the Milan Triennale of the following year – and also in more permanent settings. Perhaps the most ambitious mural cycle of the period is that in the Milan Palace of Justice, a vast construction of many rooms built between 1932 and 1940. The numerous decorative paintings were carried out between 1937 and 1939. All four signatories of the *Manifesto of Mural Painting* were among the artists involved. Also present were other Novecento artists such as Marussig. In addition to mural paintings, the decorative scheme included both low reliefs and mosaics – some by slightly unexpected hands. The young Lucio Fontana was responsible for a relief showing *Justice between the Legislative and the Executive Power*, and the veteran Futurist Gino Severini designed a number of mosaics.

The decorations follow no very precise programme, and the artists employed were allowed a good deal of liberty in interpreting the themes offered to them. Justice often appears personified (as in Fontana's relief), and there are depictions of Biblical themes, with a preference for Old Testament subjects that suggest that the law was both inflexible and inexorable, rather than for the gentler doctrines of the New Testament. The style is in general deliberately stiff and archaic, with allusions to Early Christian art (visible, for instance, in Pio Semeghini's *Christ as Legislator and Executor of the Law*), as well as to Quattrocento painting. Carrà refers unmistakably to Fra Angelico in his *Universal Judgment*, and Primo Conti to Piero della Francesca in a fresco depicting *The Justice of Heaven and Earth*.

Despite these links with the Italian past, the decorations were not well received by the judiciary. In 1939 Preda, First President of the Court of Appeal, criticized them bitterly. He alleged that the Old Testament subjects were in conflict with the new racial laws that had just been promulgated, and totally misread Semeghini's painting, going so far as to say that it placed Mussolini – symbolized in his view by the warrior figure to Christ's left – among those who had been

40. Carlo Carrà
The House, 1930

Oil on canvas
$65\frac{1}{2} \times 47\frac{5}{8}$in/166.5 × 121cm
Milan Galleria de Arte Moderna
(Artephot/Held)

brought to judgment. The decorations were for a while concealed with thick grey curtains. But Preda did not meet with universal assent, even among Fascist politicians. The Minister of Education, Giuseppe Bottai, wrote to Dino Grandi, the Minister of Justice, to say that Preda's complaints were merely a pretext, which masked an ingrained hostility to modern art: 'There remains the fact that an organ of the State has ostracized a group of works which honour the State.' Such an imbroglio would scarcely have been possible, either in Nazi Germany or in Stalinist Russia, and it is emblematic of the much greater freedom that artists enjoyed in Italy, even when, as here, they were working on official commissions.

Long before this, however, the Novecento had been in decline. Its real influence was practically extinguished by 1936. It was partly the victim of its own overwhelming success in obtaining recognition, foreign exposure and official commissions for the artists affiliated to it. This aroused the hostility of those who were excluded from the magic circle. Partly, too, it suffered from an incurable crisis of identity – the movement enlarged itself too much and thereby lost definition.

Some of its opponents evolved a theory of 'Fascist realism' based on nineteenth-century models. This might have led to an art that closely resembled the kind of thing produced under Nazi patronage. But Mussolini, though he gradually withdrew his support from the

Novecento, or at least ceased to link himself to it in quite so marked a fashion, never identified himself with this new tendency. It enjoyed only a brief moment of predominance at the very end of the decade, thanks to the change in the political climate, and to increasing German influence over Italian domestic affairs, symbolized by the passage of the racial laws already mentioned. Its high-water mark was reached with the entries for the Premio Cremona of 1940–1 (the most prestigious official prize in Italy). Competitors were asked to address themselves to set themes, such as 'Listening to one of the Duce's speeches on the radio', and this produced results that were close to both Nazi and Socialist Realist art. But at the same moment the supremacy of the Premio Cremona was being challenged by the newly founded Premio Bergamo. Here the jury pursued a totally different line – but, nevertheless, the event enjoyed strong support from Bottai. In the intellectual press the Premio Bergamo was far more amply covered than its rival.

In fact, the 1930s were a period of vigorous artistic controversy in Italy, with different groups and factions competing for public attention and frequent lively debates in newspapers and journals. Artists enjoyed many opportunities to show their work – in large exhibitions such as the Venice Biennale and the Milan Triennale, and also in private galleries. Typically, major exhibitions were the responsibility not of the State, but of different cities and communes, which retained an independence in this as in other respects reflecting the long Italian struggle for unification. The situation was thus quite unlike anything that prevailed either in Germany or in Russia at the same period.

Italian artists were able to explore a range of stylistic options almost as broad as that which existed in Paris. The two most coherent groupings in opposition to the Novecento were formed by the Abstractionists, who enjoyed a brief but vivid flowering in the middle of the decade, and by the rump of the old Futurist Movement. It perhaps comes as a surprise to discover the importance of abstraction in Italy during the 1930s. No art movement of the period has been more systematically neglected. Some of the artists concerned, chief among them Lucio Fontana, are remembered for the importance of

70

their post-war careers, others, such as Gino Ghiringelli and Manlio Rho are virtually forgotten, despite their pioneering function. One excuse for this is that pure abstraction came to Italy very belatedly – it was virtually unknown in the 1920s – and when it did come, it tended to manifest itself as an eclectic mixture of previously established styles – the overlapping planes of Cubism, the severe geometry of Piet Mondrian and *De Stijl*, and the spatial dynamism of Russian Constructivists such as Rodchenko. But there is often something sunny and classical about it that seems original, and typically Italian.

The chief focus for abstract artists was the Galleria del Milione in Milan. One of its founders was the painter-critic Carlo Belli, who had passed some time in Germany in the mid-1920s, and who had thus become acquainted with the Bauhaus and its doctrines. He appointed himself chief theoretician of the movement, and his book *Kn*, published by Edizioni del Milione in 1935, was the first treatment of abstract tendencies to appear in Italian.

The abstraction Belli promoted had two different and indeed contradictory aspects. On the one hand, it was internationalist, as abstract art had tended to be from its beginnings, and the artists were in close touch with similar tendencies elsewhere, especially with the French groups Cercle et Carré and Abstraction-Création. The Galleria del Milione, in addition to showing works by native artists, exhibited distinguished foreigners working in the same vein – works by Kandinsky, Friedrich Vordemberge-Gildewart and Josef Albers were all to be seen there in 1934. In this respect, the movement was opposed to the chauvinism of the period in Italy. On the other hand, it reconciled itself easily, from an ideological point of view, with the Fascist regime. Abstract art, taken in the context of the time, could be presented as a new art suitable to the new era Mussolini had created (the non-specific nature of purely abstract painting actually helped this argument rather than hindered it, since the new art could never be accused of negative content). Abstract artists actually found in the Duce's doctrines an echo of their own longing for rationality and order, and this piece of wishful thinking was not exposed for what it was until the political situation began to degenerate.

41. Fortunato Depero
The 1000 miles Cup, 1930

Poster
12$\frac{9}{16}$ × 10$\frac{5}{8}$ in/32 × 27cm
Galeria Museo Depero, Italy

The 'Second Futurism' of the inter-war years in Italy has been almost as much neglected as the Italian abstract art of the 1930s. The reasons for this neglect are understandable. Futurism, which had been, before World War I, perhaps the most publicized and widespread of all the avant-garde art-movements of the time, now made little stir outside its country of origin. The founder of the movement, F. T. Marinetti, continued to issue resounding manifestos, but their impact was now muffled. Marinetti's own status had become ambiguous. Formerly he had seen, and had presented, himself as a wholly revolutionary figure, concerned with political as well as with artistic change. In his political role he had been able to see himself as Mussolini's equal and rival.

Those days were now long gone. Marinetti had been constrained to join the Fascist establishment – in 1929 he accepted membership of Mussolini's restored *Accademia Italiana*, and in the same year he published a verbal 'Portrait of Mussolini' which mingles flattery with something hesitant, alienated and uneasy. It is so vivid that it is worth quoting, at least in part:

> His coat collar always turned up from an instinctive need to disguise the violent *romagnolo* words hatching their plots in his mouth.
> His right hand in his coat pocket grasps his stick like a saber straight along the muscles of his arm.
> Bent over his desk on large elbows, his arms as alert as levers, he threatens to leap across his papers at any pest or enemy. A swing of the agile torso from right to left and from left to right, to brush off trivial things. Rising to speak, he bends forward his masterful head, like a squared off projectile, a package full of good gunpowder, the cubic will of the State.

During the 1930s, unease gradually gained the upper hand, and Marinetti was courageous enough to protest at the introduction of the new Fascist racial laws in 1938.

Within Italy, the Futurist group continued to be very active, with artists such as Fortunato Depero and Enrico Prampolini, who had played only a minor role in the original movement, coming to the fore to join veterans such as Giacomo Ballà. They participated, as a group or

41, 43

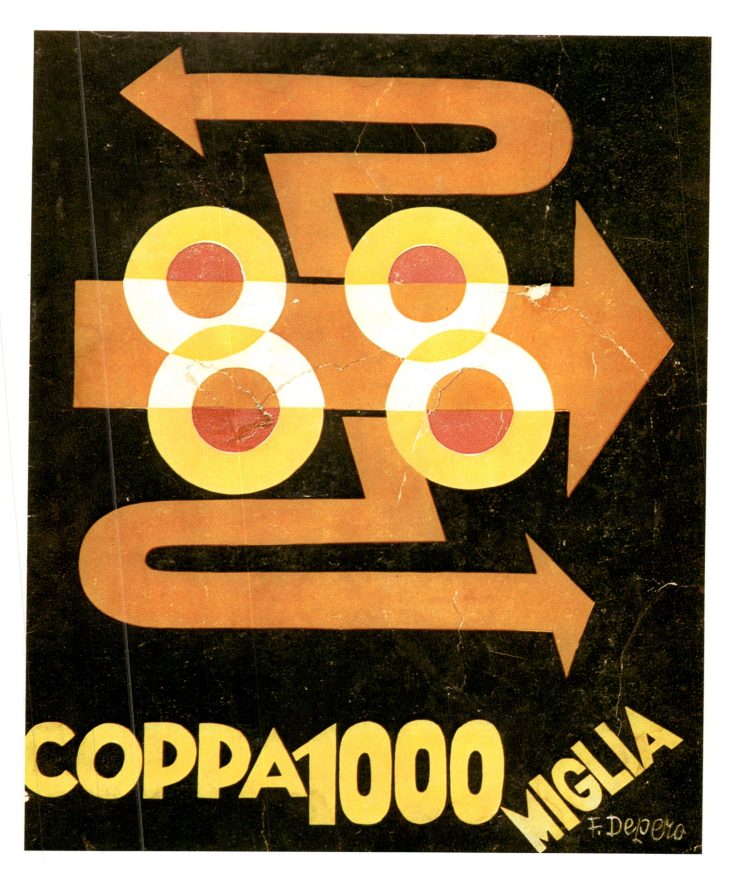

as individuals, in the big exhibitions that were a feature of the period — appearing regularly in the Venice Biennale and the Rome Quadriennale. Perhaps more than any other group they were concerned with a broad spectrum of visual expression — they were involved not only with painting and sculpture, but with architecture, advertizing and the applied arts. Their architectural projects, in particular, repay study. Those of Guido Fiorini and Nicolai Diughleroff are as prophetic in their way as those Sant'Ella created just before World War I. Like Sant'Ella's schemes, they remained unbuilt, but the Futurists did have a strong practical impact on Italian poster- and exhibition-design, both of which were of high quality at this period, at least on a level with anything being produced elsewhere in Europe and in some respects possibly superior.

Perhaps because so much of the creative energy of Futurism was now going into work of this type, the actual painting and sculpture of the second Futurism seem shallow — naïve in their continued blind worship of the machine. At this time the Futurists had become preoccupied with what they called *aeropittura* and *aerosculptura* — concepts described in a manifesto published in the *Gazetta del Populo* of Turin in September 1929:

1. The mutable perspectives offered by flight constitute an absolutely new reality which has nothing in common with the traditionally constituted reality of terrestrial perspectives.
2. The elements of this new reality have no firm point of rest and are essentially made up of this mobility.
3. The painter can only observe and depict them by taking part in their velocity.
4. To depict this new reality from on high means a profound disdain for detail, and the need to synthesize and transfigure everything.
5. All parts of the landscape seem, to the painter in flight:
a) fragmented
b) artificial
c) provisional
d) just fallen from the sky.

74

42. Carlo Levi
The Chinese Hero, 1930

Oil on canvas
$36\frac{3}{16} \times 28\frac{11}{16}$in/$92 \times 73$cm
Property of the Artist, Rome,
Collection Levi (Edizione Fabbri)

6. The following characteristics of the landscape are accentuated when seen by the painter in flight. It is:
teeming
scattered
elegant
grandiose.
7. All *aeropittura* simultaneously contains a double movement – that of the aircraft, and that of the painter's hand, holding pencil, brush or spray.
8. In *aeropittura* the painting or plastic object must be completely polycentric.
9. It will soon attain a new, extra-terrestrial spirituality of the plastic.

From its beginnings Futurism had been interested in the poetry of the machine, and, as the manifesto demonstrates, this characteristic remained with it. But one notices that, in this case, the formula is largely mechanical, despite the spiritual aspirations expressed in the

43. Enrico Prampolini
Form, Power in Space, 1932

Rome, Private Collection (Edizione
Fabbri)

final clause. Perhaps this explains some of the shallowness of effect to
be found in many of these late Futurist paintings. There is also the
feeling that, in some cases, the Futurist artists of the 1930s were
attempting effects that were really more suitable to film. One Futurist
sculptor of the period, Renato di Bosso, actually made a sculpture in
carved and painted wood which represents the *Descent of a Parachutist*
(1933).

These groupings – the Novecento, the Abstractionists, and the
Futurists, by no means exhaust the list of art-styles in Mussolini's Italy.
In figurative painting, there was a very wide range of possibilities,

extending even to the tempered Expressionism of an artist like Carlo Levi, which can be compared to the more fervent and violent version of the same style being practised in Paris by Chaïm Soutine. Another, and slightly younger artist who for a time formed part of this Expressionist current was Renato Guttuso. His meteoric and controversial career exemplifies both the degree of freedom offered to artists by Mussolini's Italy, and the way in which the nature of the regime, lax and tolerant though it was in some respects, inexorably pushed them into opposition. Guttuso's early career as a painter lies entirely within the decade under discussion. Born in Sicily in 1912, he at first began to study law, then decided to dedicate himself entirely to art. In 1931 he exhibited in the Rome Quadriennale, and then in a mixed exhibition at the Galleria del Milione in Milan in the following year. His penchant for dramatic realism was already apparent – early influences included van Gogh and Oskar Kokoschka, and later he was to feel the impact of Picasso's *Guernica*, which was not merely a lesson in style, but something attuned to his political sympathies. Significantly Guttuso owed much of his early renown to successes in the Premio Bergamo. His *Flight from Etna* won third prize in 1940, and in 1942 his *Crucifixion*, after a violent controversy between conservatives and innovators, was accorded second place. Guttuso's hatred of Fascism was never in question – during the war he fought with the partisans and later published an album of drawings recording his experiences under the title *Gott mit Uns*. But it is also true to say that the career he pursued in the 1930s, controversial, but marked by moments of official and public success, would have been impossible under the other totalitarian regimes.

44

Guttuso, however, does not really seem the typical artist of the period. That honour should perhaps be divided between the painter Giorgio Morandi and the two sculptors Giacomo Manzù and Marino Marini. In the case of the two latter it is often forgotten how important a part of their careers was spent under Fascism.

In 1930, Morandi reached the age of forty – his style had been fully formed for nearly a decade. In his youth he had been influenced by the Futurists (he knew Umberto Boccioni personally), but also by an artist

44. Renato Guttuso
The Crucifixion, 1942

Oil on canvas
$78\frac{11}{16} \times 78\frac{11}{16}$in/$200 \times 200$cm
Guttuso (Scala)

who had gone in a very different direction – Cézanne. A little later he was attracted into the orbit of de Chirico's *pittura metafisica*. His later work, especially his still lifes (which made up the majority of his production) retained an echo of the metaphysical style – they combine extreme quietude with a barely detectable sense of alienation. Nevertheless, they were painted in a very different fashion. Rather than being dry, they were done with paint that seemed creamy and almost edible. From the early 1920s Morandi confined himself to small formats and a very restricted range of subject-matter – apart from still lifes, he painted only landscapes. In the still lifes themselves he used the **45** same subjects, mostly bottles and vases, over and over again. Whatever Morandi painted, the subject was only a pretext. His work was a long meditation about the way in which art is made.

It would be easy to categorize Morandi as an artist who found a way to survive under a dictatorship. But in fact he did better than that. Under Mussolini he was far from being neglected. In 1930 he was given an official post – Professor of Graphic Arts in the Bologna Academy of

Fine Arts. He retained it until 1956. He exhibited at both the Venice Biennale and the Rome Quadriennale. In 1939, he was awarded third prize at the Quadriennale, and there was a special one-man show of his work within the main exhibition.

Manzù and Marini pursued quietly successful careers in much the same fashion. Manzù, who was born in 1908, did not begin to emerge as an artistic personality until the 1930s – his first one-man show was held in Milan, at the Galleria del Milione, in 1932. His earliest work was inspired by the Renaissance, and also by his discovery of Etruscan art. Later influences were Medardo Rosso, with his daring pictorial effects, and Rodin, whom he discovered only in 1936 on his second trip to Paris. The first, in 1929, had been cut short by lack of money. During the second half of the 1930s Manzù enjoyed considerable success. He had a major one-man show at a private gallery in Rome in 1937 and followed this by making a big impact at the Venice Biennale of 1938. In 1941 he was appointed to teach sculpture at the Accademia Albertina in Turin.

45. Giorgio Morandi
Still Life, c. 1930

Oil on canvas
$18\frac{1}{2} \times 17\frac{11}{16}$in/47 × 45cm
Private Collection
(Artephot/Himatallah)

Manzù's art holds a delicate balance between what is academic and what is visibly modern. A number of his figures seem at first glance to have a slight awkwardness of proportion or stance. The unexpected rhythms he gives to what are to all appearances naturalistic forms help to make his sculpture memorable. Etruscan sculpture, struggling to learn the lessons of Greek art, but still imbued with its own native feeling, shows the same characteristics.

The same can be said about the sculptures of Marino Marini, Manzù's contemporary and rival. Marini was seven years older than Manzù, but his artistic formation was much the same – Paris, the influence of Medardo Rosso, and that of the Etruscans. He rebelled, perhaps more consciously than Manzù, against the heavy classicism of Maillol, and he showed less interest in the Renaissance. A further influence on his work, not always cited, was the sculpture of T'ang China, particularly the pottery tomb figures of horses and riders, which seem to have inspired Marini's own celebrated series of horsemen.

Like Manzù, Marini was extremely successful in Mussolini's Italy, being awarded the first prize for sculpture in the Second Rome Quadriennale of 1935. His links with the regime were perhaps closer than those of Manzù – for example, he made a figure of *Italia Armed* for the exhibition that celebrated the tenth anniversary of Fascism in 1932. He followed the example of Morandi and Manzù in remaining part of the art-education system. From 1929 to 1940 he was professor of sculpture at the Scuola d'Arte in Monza, leaving this post for another and more senior one at the Accademia del Brera in Milan.

These three examples demonstrate that creative artists of considerable quality were able to live and work under Mussolini's regime, apparently without feeling that they were thereby forced to compromise their art. Only the war obliged the two sculptors, Manzù in particular, to adopt a different attitude. The works Manzù produced during the German occupation of Italy allude openly to the horror of the times and condemn this, not the Fascist past. In a series of *Depositions* and *Crucifixions*, the executioners appear as German soldiers.

The work of all three artists indicates that the reassessment of Modernism which took place in Italy during the inter-war years was

46. Giorgio de Chirico
Self-portrait, c. 1935

Rome, Private Collection (Edizione Fabbri)

47. Giorgio de Chirico
Two Horses by the Seashore,
c. 1931–4

Oil on canvas
25¼ × 31¼in/64 × 79.5cm
Sotheby's

46, 47

something that arose spontaneously. Morandi, Manzù and Marini are nevertheless still indelibly marked by the Modernist spirit – any conservatism we may find in their work is only relative. The kind of eclecticism Manzù and Marini practised is a twentieth-century phenomenon, different in kind from the eclecticism of the *artistes pompiers* of a century earlier. It relies on our recognition of the elements used, and our further recognition that they are slightly incongruous. Art of this kind is the produce of the *musée imaginaire* which Malraux was later to identify as a primary invention of the Modernist epoch.

An artist who took the past more literally (one cannot perhaps say more seriously) was Giorgio de Chirico, once the most radical innovator in Italian art. De Chirico based himself outside Italy during

82

the 1930s, living mostly in Paris, but still maintained close contact with the Italian art-world and exhibited frequently in various Italian cities. His conduct during the years that followed the brief flowering of *pittura metafisica* has provided a puzzle for art historians, and fertile subject-matter for moralists of all kinds. He noisily denounced his original commitment to Modernism, and at the same time produced replicas of earlier compositions, sometimes attempting to pass these off as authentic works of an earlier epoch. On occasion he denounced genuine early works as forgeries. His new style was based on the Old Masters, and in the 1930s became increasingly Realist. The paintings he produced were often Renaissance or Baroque pastiches (among them self-portraits in which he implicitly compared himself to great masters of the past such as Raphael). But there were also elements he had used even in his 'metaphysical' period – for example, borrowings from Pompeian frescoes. This strain is evident in the illustrations he made in 1934 for Cocteau's *Mythologie*.

Until recently it has been usual to dismiss all de Chirico's later efforts as things that show only the sad remnants of a great talent. Now there is an inclination to class him as a premature anti-Modernist, the chief predecessor of the *pittura colta* which has become fashionable in Italy during the 1980s. This is perhaps to do him too much justice, rather than too little. The uneven work of his later years, and the somewhat strained polemics with which he accompanied it, demonstrate the dilemmas that assailed many artists in the inter-war years – the longing for some kind of stability and order after a period of extreme turbulence and danger. De Chirico's work is not 'Fascist painting' in any specific way, but it springs from the same trauma that provided Mussolini with his political success, and led so many artists of quality to work both with and for his regime.

The Mexican Muralists

One new phenomenon in the 1930s was the way in which Modernism began to exert an influence beyond the boundaries of Europe and North America. The ground it lost in Russia and in Nazi Germany was made up elsewhere, particularly in Latin America. The Latin American nation that first felt the impact of Modernism was Mexico, and by the beginning of the decade Mexico was starting to exert a potent influence of its own, especially within the American hemisphere. The interest in murals, which was so vigorously in evidence in the United States during the period, owed a good deal to the example that had already been set south of the border.

The Mexican mural movement had made an abortive start as early as 1910, when six artists headed by Dr Atl (Gerardo Murillo) were commissioned to decorate the Anfiteatro Bolívar, a new auditorium in the National Preparatory School, formerly the Jesuit College of San Ildefonso, in Mexico City. One member of the *équipe* was later to become famous as a leading muralist. His name was José Clemente Orozco. The subject of the murals was the History of Human Evolution. The project was halted by the outbreak of the Mexican Revolution under Francesco Madero.

During the turbulent decade that followed, the poet-philosopher José Vasconcelos briefly held office as Minister of Education, before being forced into a five-year exile in the United States. Vasconcelos was perhaps the first to espouse the idea that Mexico needed a new revolutionary art that would address itself directly to the people. Vasconcelos's ideas were not entirely forgotten while he was in exile, and in 1919 a Congress of Soldier-Artists was held in Guadalajara to discuss 'new orientations of art and culture'.

General Alvaro Obregón became President of Mexico in 1920, and Vasconcelos returned to office as Minister of Education. With the aid of Dr Atl and others, he immediately launched a nationalist Mexican art movement, which looked beyond the Colonial period and sought roots in native Indian culture. Mural painting had been an important aspect of Mexican art in the Pre-Columbian epoch, and this, in addition to the fact that murals addressed themselves directly to a popular audience, was another reason for wishing to revive this means of

48. Diego Rivera
Class Struggle (detail), 1935

Palacio Nacional Mexico
(Edimedia)

expression. The first mural commission was given in June 1920 to an artist named Robert Montenegro. News of what Vasconcelos was doing travelled abroad, and in 1921 the young David Alfaro Siqueiros published his *Manifesto a los Plásticos de América* in Barcelona. This vigorously supported the notion that the quintessential revolutionary art was monumental mural painting.

The man who first put all these ideas into practical effect was neither Montenegro nor Siqueiros, but Diego Rivera. Rivera, who had spent a long period in France working in an orthodox Cubist style, arrived in Mexico in 1921, and was commissioned to decorate the same Anfiteatro Bolívar where work had been cut short in 1910. His *Creation* mural, decorating the stage, was the true start of the Mexican mural movement of the 1920s and 1930s, despite the fact that there was little which was specifically Mexican about its style. Rivera was soon joined at the National Preparatory School by Jean Charlot, a young Frenchman deeply interested in Pre-Columbian art. His studies were to have a decisive influence. They prepared the way for the emergence of a distinctively national style. Also part of the team were

49. Jean Charlot
The Fall of Tenochtillán
(detail), 1922–3

Pedro Rojas (Visual Arts Library

50. Diego Rivera
*Man with Animal's Head
Stabbing the Conqueror in
Armour* (detail), 1929–30

Mural at Palacio de Cortés
Cuernavaca, Morelos (Edimedia)

49

Orozco and Siqueiros. The artists worked for artisans' wages, rediscovering the techniques of mural painting as they progressed. Some of their imagery was highly controversial, and in June 1924 the murals by Orozco and Siqueiros were attacked and defaced by students at the School. Vasconcelos resigned, and only Rivera continued to paint, a pistol stuck in his belt. In 1926, when the controversy died down a little, Orozco was able to return and complete the task allotted to him. A few murals were also painted at locations outside Mexico City: in Guadalajara and at the Agricultural School at Chapingo.

By the late 1920s, the first phase of the mural movement was more or less over. Rivera emerged as the undisputed leader of the muralists, chiefly because he was able to go on painting more or less continuously, apart from a brief and disillusioning visit to Soviet Russia in 1927–8. The others dispersed. Charlot turned to research into Mayan art in Yucatán. Orozco went to the United States. Siqueiros followed Rivera to Russia and then became increasingly involved in politics. He was not to paint another mural in Mexico till 1939. One reason why Rivera was able to continue was that he attracted outside patronage. The murals in the Palacio de Cortés in Cuernavaca, painted in 1929–30 and now among his most famous works, were commissioned and paid for by Dwight D. Morrow, the United States Ambassador to Mexico.

The style Rivera evolved for his mural work had very mixed origins. In its fundamental structure, it owed much to the Cubism Rivera had practised in Paris before his return to Mexico. For example, Rivera habitually makes use of a shallow picture-space and tip-tilted planes. Forms are often crammed into compartments that seem too small for them. But Rivera discarded Cubist ambiguity in favour of both formal and narrative clarity – for the first time since the defeat of the *artistes-pompiers*, narrative values were wholeheartedly restored to art. Because he was a nationalist Rivera made a conscious search for national roots. He found these not only in the Pre-Columbian paintings to which he had been guided by Charlot's researches, but in the art of the colonial period, and in Mexican popular painting, for example in the folk paintings that adorned the walls of *pulquerías* or

4, 50

51, 48, 53

51. Diego Rivera
Aztec Medecine and Modern Medecine (detail), 1929

Fresco at the Ministry of Social Security
The Aztec clinic Health Ministry
(Edimedia)

88

drink shops. The colonial influence in Rivera's work is often overlooked. From colonial art he took his hard-edged, slightly wooden forms – these derive, if rather distantly, from the religious paintings of the studio of Francisco de Zurbarán which were exported in great quantity to the Spanish Indies. His compositional schematas often owe much to the religious art of the Baroque period.

Another artist whom Rivera seems to have examined closely is 'Le Douanier' (Henri Rousseau). Rousseau's jungle scenes find a clear echo in some details of Rivera's frescoes for the Palacio de Cortés – for instance, the scene showing a tree being felled in order to make a bridge.

Rivera's success is measurable in his power to seize the imagination, not only of his Mexican compatriots, but that of foreigners as well. Despite his unconcealed distaste for the gringos and everything they stood for, he became celebrated and sought after in the United States. In 1930 he was invited to San Francisco to paint murals in the San Francisco Stock Exchange Club and in the San Francisco School of Fine Arts.

Stylistically Orozco and Siqueiros differed considerably from Rivera. Orozco, now ranked by many as the greatest of the Mexican muralists, was slightly older than Rivera, and lacked the latter's experience of Europe. An early influence on his work was the popular **52** illustrator José Guadalupe Posada (1852–1913), whose gallows humour and sense of irony are peculiarly Mexican. Orozco too made his beginnings as an illustrator and caricaturist, and found plenty of employment for his satirical gifts during the years of the Revolution. Disillusioned by events in Mexico, he left the country in 1917 and went to America, working in San Francisco as a sign painter and in New York painting the faces of dolls. When he came back to Mexico to participate in the mural movement, his experience as a caricaturist made itself felt in the savage social satires he provided as his share of the work in the National Preparatory School.

Yet Orozco, unlike Rivera and Siqueiros, never became a Marxist, and often expressed deep scepticism about the whole political process. His early murals already show the Expressionist strain that was to

52. José Guadalupe Posada
Cyclists in the late nineteenth century

Drawing
Inter-American Fund

appear even more clearly in his mature compositions. Wounded by his treatment at the National Preparatory School, and by the government's apparent unwillingness to support him, Orozco retreated to the United States in 1927 and did not return to Mexico until the mid-1930s. A letter written to Jean Charlot from New York in 1928 shows his resentment at the way in which Rivera seemed to take all the credit for the success of the mural movement.

> Diegoff Riveritch Romanoff: Still a big threat to us. As I told your mother when I answered her letter, the idea that we are all his disciples is very well entrenched here. To talk about 'Indians' 'revolution', 'Mexican renaissance', 'folk arts', '*retablos*' etc., etc., is to talk about Rivera . . . ['Orozco', catalogue of an exhibition held at the Museum of Modern Art (Oxford 1980), p. 42].

Nevertheless, Orozco retained his faith in the principles upon which Mexican muralism had been founded, as he made plain in a manifesto published in January 1929:

> The highest, the most logical, the purest and strongest form of painting is the mural. In this form alone is it one with the other arts – with all the others.
>   It is, too, the most disinterested form, for it cannot be made a matter of private gain; it cannot be hidden away for the benefit of a certain privileged few.
>   It is for the people. It is for ALL. ['Orozco', catalogue, p. 46].

Whereas Orozco withdrew to America when the first phase of the Mexican mural movement was over, Siqueiros threw himself into **58**

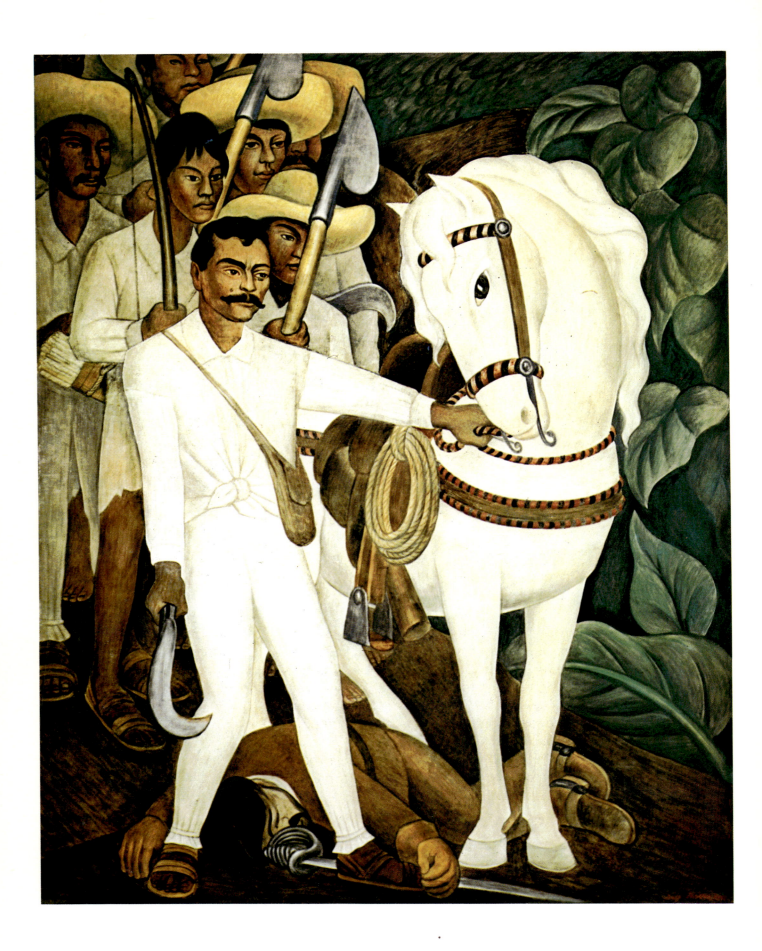

revolutionary politics, devoting himself to the Communist Party. He organized the Federation of Miners in the province of Jalisco, and in 1928 made the journey to Russia, without the disillusioning effects this had on Rivera. A year later he went to South America as a workers' delegate. In 1931, back in Mexico, he was arrested during a clash at a political demonstration and spent a period in gaol, and a further period under house-arrest at Taxco.

At the beginning of the 1930s all the original leaders of the mural movement were at least temporarily away from the country. Nevertheless, the impulse to decorate public walls remained, and the Mexican government once again began to give commissions, using a new generation of artists. The most significant début was that of Rufino Tamayo who, in 1933, produced his first mural, now largely repainted and altered, at the then Museo Nacional de Antropología y

54. José Clemente Orozco
Zapatistas, 1931

Mural
45 × 55in/114.3 × 140cm
Museum of Modern Art, New York
(Visual Arts Library)

53. Diego Rivera
Zapata, 1931

Fresco
94 × 74in/239 × 188in
Museum of Modern Art, New York
(Visual Arts Library)

Historia. It was an important début not least because it signalized an impulse to revolt against certain things that the first generation of muralists took for granted. Tamayo later said:

> [Though] I belonged to a generation that was too young at that time to become leaders of the Mexican pictorial movement that was just beginning, I, nevertheless, disapproved decidedly of the slant that the mature artists were giving our painting. Although the painting of that initial period revealed some distinguishing qualities, the preoccupation of its authors to produce, above all, art that was Mexican, even though in appearance only, led them to fall into the picturesque and to be careless of the really plastic problems. When I saw what was happening, and being convinced that our painting should be Mexican in essence, but without omitting the technical side of what was being neglected, I reacted strongly against the established norms and together with other colleagues, initiated a movement tending to return our painting to its pure qualities. [Carlos Merida, *Modern Mexican Artists*, 2nd ed. (New York 1968)].

Opposed to Tamayo's individualism, however, was the growth of the collectivist principle. Increasingly, mural commissions were given, not to individuals but to groups, often of very young and inexperienced artists. Sometimes these groups were organized into so-called Cultural Missions which rapidly provided decorations for schools, outdoor theatres and other new buildings under construction throughout Mexico. Many of these decorations have not survived, and none count among the major achievements of Mexican muralism.

Meanwhile Rivera and Orozco were far from idle in their North American exile. As soon as he arrived in San Francisco, Rivera gathered a cosmopolitan retinue around him – it included an ex-Mountie from Canada and the heir to an English earldom. His mural at the San Francisco School of Fine Arts was simultaneously a manifesto and a joke. It shows the artist and his assistants perched on a *trompe-l'oeil* scaffold, painting a fresco of a worker on what appears to be the actual wall of the room. Rivera's enormous backside is prominent – he was a very fat as well as a very tall man. The mural caused a gratifying commotion and did Rivera's growing fame no damage. After a brief return to Mexico he was invited to New York for a retrospective exhibition of his work at the Museum of Modern Art – the Museum's second one-man exhibition (they had kicked off with Matisse). The invitation to Rivera was backed by members of the Rockefeller and Aldrich families, who had large investments in Latin America. When he arrived, Rivera was lionized. One of his new friends was Mrs John D. Rockefeller, born Abby Aldrich. She asked him to paint a new version of a satirical mural already completed in Mexico for the wall of her dining-room. Entitled *Night of the Rich*, it shows John D. Rockefeller, J. P. Morgan and Henry Ford dining on ticker-tape. Rivera prudently refused. The retrospective was both a critical and a popular success: it attracted over 50,000 visitors. The *New York Sun* called Rivera 'the most talked-about man this side of the Atlantic'.

Rivera's next stop was Detroit, where he was invited to provide murals for the Detroit Institute of Arts. These proved even more controversial than his San Francisco commission – they were described locally as 'a heartless hoax on (Rivera's) capitalist employers' and 'a travesty of the spirit of Detroit'. Once again Rivera emerged with his reputation unscathed, and proceeded to his next and most prestigious task – murals for the new Rockefeller Center in New York. The theme chosen by his patrons was 'Man at the Crossroads looking with Hope and High Vision to the Choosing of a New and Better Future'. Flushed with success Rivera could not resist pushing his patrons too far. It was not merely that he filled the composition with the colour red, but he introduced an extremely recognizable portrait of Lenin. Work on the mural was abruptly terminated, and Rivera was fired after being paid his fee in full.

He lingered on in New York, painting a series of murals at the New Workers' School (run by a Communist but anti-Stalinist organization). These took the form of twenty-one movable panels in a soon-to-be-demolished building – and then two more small panels for the headquarters of the New York Trotskyites. Finally the funds he had received from the Rockefellers were exhausted, and so was the patience of his wife Frida Kahlo, who longed for Mexico. They made a somewhat inglorious departure for home in December 1933.

Orozco worked in the United States with much less fanfare, but the work he did there was much more important for his own development as an artist than Rivera's American commissions were to him. It was 1930 before he, too, was asked to paint a mural in the United States, though he had returned there three years earlier. His first patrons were the students of Pomona College at Claremont, California, urged on by an admirer of Orozco's – their Professor of Spanish Civilization. The subject chosen was *Prometheus*, and it shows Orozco's powerful Expressionist style at full stretch. The Pomona mural was followed by a commission to paint a series of panels for the cafeteria of the New School for Social Research in New York – a place where Thomas Hart Benton was also to work. Orozco did the job for subsistence wages – a great contrast to the high fees Rivera was being paid by American patrons at the same period. Orozco did somewhat better when he went to Dartmouth College, Hanover, New Hampshire, where he worked from 1932 to 1934. For Dartmouth College library he planned a cycle that would give physical embodiment to his vision of the progress of civilization on the American continent. It was an epic theme, and he gave it its full dimensions. One of Orozco's admirers was the Russian film director Sergei Eisenstein, who was familiar with his Preparatory School murals at first hand. On seeing the booklet that illustrated the Dartmouth College murals, Eisenstein wrote the following:

> Orozco's progress: Dartmouth. There it was the terrible. Super-human passions. Social outcry. And amongst these social carica-tures, a handsome young boy, with that ease which only Americans have, was sitting peacefully in that room overflowing with a social tumult of colours. Orozco at least is not going to compromise. ['Orozco', catalogue, p. 68].

Siqueiros also spent much time in the United States during the 1930s, despite his loudly professed hatred of American imperialism. His imprisonment was followed by an extremely successful exhibition held in Mexico City of the paintings he had done in the penitentiary

56, 57

55

55. José Clemente Orozco *Mexican Modern Human Sacrifice from the mural series*, detail of The Epic of American Civilization,

1932–4 commissioned by the Trustees of Dartmouth College

Courtesy of the Trustees of Dartmouth College

56. José Clemente Orozco
Scientist/Worker/Artist
(detail)

Mural for the New York New
School of Social Research

and while under house-arrest at Taxco. Taxco was important for another reason. During his time there Siqueiros got to know Eisenstein, and the latter inspired him, not only with an enthusiasm for photomontage, but with ideas about the use of distortion and multiple perspective — things that would help to make mural painting the equivalent of the new art of the cinema.

When Siqueiros arrived in Los Angeles in 1932, having made Mexico too hot to hold him for the time being, he was commissioned to do two murals, one at the Chouinard School of Art, Los Angeles and the other at the Plaza Art Center. He dispatched these jobs in short order. In a lecture delivered to the John Reed Club of Hollywood in September 1932, he made it plain first that he regarded mural painting as an essentially collective art, and secondly that he felt the painter should take advantage of all the techniques modern technology made available to him. He recommended the use of the spray gun, the blow torch, the electric projector (as an aid to tracing the design on the wall), and of cement ready mixed in various colours. For Siqueiros modern mechanical methods corresponded to revolutionary convictions and allowed them to be expressed as an integral part of the aesthetic effect.

From Los Angeles Siqueiros went to Uruguay and Argentina, producing a mural in Buenos Aires in collaboration with a group of Argentinian artists, and triggering off a subsidiary mural movement there. He held a successful exhibition in New York after his visit to Argentina — this brought his work to the attention of important American collectors — and then returned to Mexico, where in 1935 he

engaged in some comically inconclusive polemics with Rivera, based less on their aesthetic than their political differences as supporters of two different brands of Communism. Ever restless, he then went to New York once more, where in 1935–6 he ran an Experimental Workshop attended by Jackson Pollock among others. Here Siqueiros did not encourage the use of synthetic paints (his students nicknamed him 'Signor Duco'), but demonstrated a version of the drip technique Pollock was later to make famous. The Workshop was short-lived. Siqueiros could not resist the pull of the Spanish Civil War. In 1937 he took himself off to join the Spanish Republican Army, and was promptly commissioned as a Colonel.

I have chronicled the activities of the leading Mexican muralists in the United States in so much detail for two reasons. One is that the work they did in America formed an integral part of their development as artists. The other is that the story demonstrates the fact that, despite its ultra-nationalist stance, Mexican muralism was at least partly dependent on patronage from outside Mexico itself. This dependency was not merely monetary: Mexican artists needed the

57. José Clemente Orozco
Puerto, Lenin and the Bolshevik Revolution (detail) 1929–31

Mural for the New York New School of Social Research

59

99

approval of American critics and patrons to consolidate their position with their own public at home. It must be said that the Americans who supported Mexican art often (though not invariably) showed a remarkable ability to swallow political and social viewpoints very different from their own.

Because of this dependency on outsiders — itself an ironic proof of the cultural colonialism they condemned — the Mexicans differed from the 'nationalist' artists at work during the 1930s in Soviet Russia, Nazi Germany, or even in Fascist Italy — though Mussolini's government did make great efforts to enhance the reputation of Italian painters and sculptors abroad.

The Mexicans gave something to the United States in return for what they got. The many murals painted there during the 1930s were initially inspired by the Mexican example. In the case of Siqueiros the link with American art was closer and more intimate still, though he had the least in the way of actual achievement to show for his stay in the United States. The experiments he conducted during his years in the United States provided Abstract Expressionism with part of its impetus, and it is also possible to see him as being, thanks to the ideas he absorbed from Eisenstein, one of the ancestors of Pop Art, Abstract Expressionism's successor and rival.

When Rivera and Orozco returned to Mexico, their prestige enhanced by what they had achieved while absent, they were immediately commissioned to paint a fresco apiece in the huge Art Deco Palacio de Bellas Artes in Mexico City. Rivera chose to recreate his lost Rockefeller Center mural. Its balanced quasi-scientific style made it more didactic and less romantic than many of his compositions in the past. Orozco's fresco, *Catharsis*, facing Rivera's, is more stormy and dramatic: it is a cry of rage against the brutality of mankind.

After completing his Bellas Artes commission, Rivera went back to working at the Palacio Nacional on the Zócalo, the main square of Mexico City, where he had left a staircase mural incomplete on his departure for America. After finishing this, he produced yet more frescoes there. Familiar figures from the new Mexican iconography appear; the Officer, the Banker, the Priest, Demagogues, and a

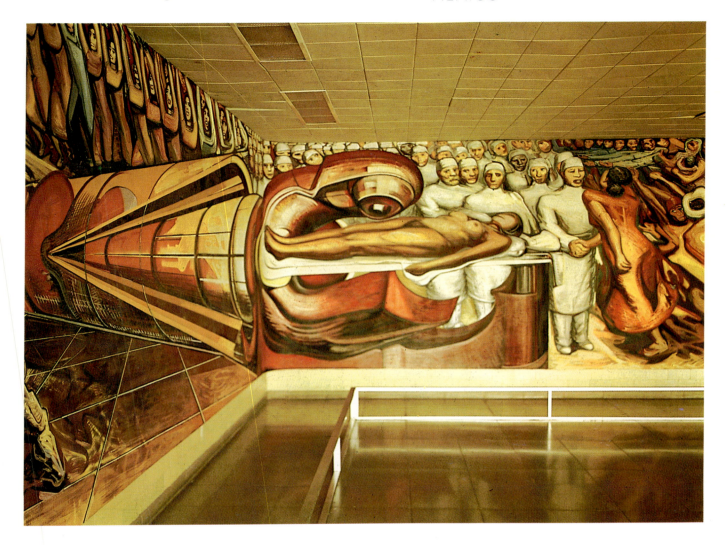

suitably colossal likeness of Marx pointing towards the future.

Siqueiros returned to Mexico from Spain, and in 1939 painted his first mural in his native country since the 1920s. It covers the walls of a stairway in the headquarters of the Union of Electricians in Mexico City, and shows machinery devouring humans, while an orator directs the proceedings through a microphone.

The most significant achievement of Mexican muralism in the late 1930s was the work done by Orozco in Guadalajara, capital of his own native province of Jalisco. The work done at this period represents the peak of his achievement as an artist, and the peak of Mexican mural painting as a whole. The largest cycle of paintings, 1938–9, is in the deconsecrated chapel of the Hospicio Cabañas – an orphanage. The building is part of an early nineteenth-century complex designed by Mexico's greatest neo-classical architect, Manuel Tolsá. Its severe style

58. David Alfaro Siqueiros
Celebration of the Future Victory of Medical Science over Cancer (detail)

Medical Centre, Mexico City
(Pedro Rojas/Visual Arts Library)

101

59. David Alfaro Siqueiros
Echo of a Scream, 1937

Duco on wood
48 × 36in/121.9 × 91.4cm
Collection, The Museum of Modern
Art, New York. Gift of Edward
M.M. Warburg

complements the force of Orozco's images. His compositions differ from more traditional murals in a number of ways – in their broad painterliness, as well as in the actual compositional formulae. Sometimes the available spaces are packed with struggling figures, but often there is only a single figure or just a symbol, rendered with overwhelming boldness. The themes treated in the cycle are complex. Orozco aimed to show the changes Mexico had undergone in the centuries since the Spanish Conquest. The general tone is not

optimistic, though Orozco continued to affirm the possibilities open   **60**
to the human spirit. Neither the pre-Conquest Indian world nor the
Conquest itself are viewed at all sentimentally. The Indian world is
macabre and violent, rather than idyllic; the Conquest is equally
violent, in addition to being aggressive and acquisitive. Christian
spirituality is shown being used as a weapon. A parallel is also drawn
between the Conquest and modern warfare. The horse, which gave   **54**
the conquistadors such an advantage over the Indians, is seen as the
equivalent of the modern tank. Orozco offered no relief in the modern
world to balance this gloomy view of history. The masses are depicted
as being dehumanized; the Mexican Revolution as something that
stopped halfway.

Orozco's verdict on the Mexican mural movement was as uncom-
promising as the work he produced:

> Having studied the themes in modern Mexican mural paintings, we
> find the following facts: all the painters began with subjects derived
> from traditional iconography, either Christian or Frankish, and
> often literally copied them.
>
> In the first murals we find the bearded or beardless figure of the
> Pantocrator, virgins, angels, saint-burials, martyrs and even the
> Virgin of Guadalupe. All that was missing was the Sacred Heart of
> Jesus and Saint Anthony.
>
> After the first period three perfectly definable trends appeared:
> the Indian trend in its two variants, the archaic and the colourfully
> folkloric – the Olympian, Toltec or Aztec and the types and
> traditions of the present Indian artists with all their magnificent
> richness of colour.
>
> The second trend has an historical content in which Mexican
> history, preferably the Conquest, is dealt with; history is shown
> from contradictory and opposing viewpoints. Those who are heroes
> in one mural are villains in another.
>
> And lastly, there is the great trend of revolutionary socialist
> propaganda, in which there continues to appear, with surprising
> persistency, Christian iconography. Its interminable martyrs, per-

secutions, miracles, prophets, saint-fathers, evangelists, supreme pontiffs, Last Judgments, hells and heavens, the just and sinners, heretics, schismatics, triumphs of the Church, Byzantine discussions, iconoclastic emperors, Councils, Savonarolas, inquisitors, Jesuits, Hope and Charity, the Holy Sepulchre and even the Crusades. All these are superficially modernized; perhaps rifles and machine-guns in place of bows and arrows; aeroplanes instead of angels; flying atomic bombs in place of divine damnation and a confused and fantastic paradise very difficult to define.

To all this outdated religious imagery very 19th century liberal symbols are added. Freedom with its Phrygian cap and the indispensable broken chains; Democracy; Peace; Blindfolded Justice carrying its sword and scales; The Nation; torches, stars, palms and olives; heraldic or symbolic animals, including eagles, lions, tigers, horses and serpents. Very ancient symbols of the 'Bourgeoisie, enemy of progress' type, still play a prominent part in murals, represented by pot-bellied toffs in top hats, or by pigs, jackals, dragons or other monsters, so well-known and familiar that they are as inoffensive as the plumed serpent. ['Orozco', catalogue, p. 116 (from a text prepared for Orozco's retrospective exhibition at the Palacio de Bellas Artes in 1947)].

Orozco's verdict on his colleagues, which was also to some extent a verdict on himself, may seem unduly harsh, but it focuses unerringly on the main weakness of the products of the Mexican mural movement – the uneasy combination of traditionalism and modernism, with the two elements retaining separate identities rather than fusing together to make a genuine whole. The difficulties that afflicted the Mexican mural painters affected all the 'public' artists of the time. They seem to have felt that, to address a mass audience successfully, they needed to pour their new wine into reassuringly old bottles. Yet there was an important difference between public art in Mexico and public art in either Germany or Russia, though, like these, Mexico was a one-party state with a revolutionary political programme. The Mexicans remained remarkably free to express their own meanings, as Orozco's Hospicio Cabañas murals demonstrate. If the Mexican muralists

60. José Clemente Orozco
The Five Phases of Man,
(detail) 1936

Mexico

employed the clichés of the past, it was done, not under orders, but of their own volition. As a result, even where they employed conventional symbols and formulations, these tended to be used in unconventional or even downright eccentric ways. These individual eccentricities help to keep their work alive for us today.

The Mexican mural movement, though widely publicized as a producer of 'democratic' art, remained quite narrowly based. Between 1905 and 1969, which may be taken as the extreme limits of the mural movement, 1,286 murals were produced by only 289 artists. Obviously Mexico contained many more painters than this. But the mural movement was so effective in making reputations for those who

participated in it that it is mostly these artists who are remembered today. One exception, a painter who never attempted mural painting, was Rivera's wife, Frida Kahlo. Kahlo was largely self-taught, and her paintings are an anguished autobiography, with a high proportion of self-portraits. She suffered lifelong pain from the effects of an accident sustained while she was still a girl, and had frequent spells in hospital. Her paintings are small in scale, and are often based on Mexican folk models, chiefly the votive paintings made to be hung in churches. In some ways Kahlo remained more truly faithful to a genuinely Mexican tradition and sensibility than the ambitious muralists who were her contemporaries. Yet, both because of the small scale on which she worked, and because of Kahlo's role as consort to Mexico's most celebrated modern artist, she was slow in gaining recognition. Today, thanks to a bizarre reversal of fortune, Kahlo is the subject of an outstanding modern biography, while Rivera awaits the definitive study he undoubtedly deserves.

61

It is easy to pick holes in what the muralists did, and to demonstrate that their work was often derivative and lazy – a backsliding from strict Modernist principles. At the same time, however, they provided the Mexican audience with a genuine focus for feelings about the nature of national identity.

61. Frida Kahlo
Self-Portrait, 1940

$15\frac{3}{4} \times 11$ in/40×28cm
Museum of Modern Art, New York
(Visual Arts Library)

The Middle Age of the École de Paris

Nazi Germany and Soviet Russia might rebel against the tenets of Modernism during the 1930s, but it remained dominant in France. It was the École de Paris that set the standard for democratic Europe, and to some extent for the United States as well. Yet even here there was a subtle shift of alignments. French Modernism of the 1930s was not – how could it be? – the Modernism that had flourished so vigorously throughout the pioneering decades before and during World War I. The major artists who had created the Modern Movement in Paris during that period were for the most part alive and hard at work. But the magic circle no longer existed – many of the chief figures had gone their separate ways. The urge to change and renew everything was no longer as forceful as it had been to begin with. At the same time, the artists themselves, now men in late-middle age, had become established, and had gained at least a limited degree of public acceptance. Though Paris remained the irreplaceable centre, a number of the most celebrated artists no longer lived there – Pierre Bonnard and Henri Matisse, for example, found the South of France a more congenial place to live and work.

The two painters had something more in common with one another than this. In art, both were arch hedonists, and during the 1920s both had sought some kind of accommodation with public taste. Bonnard, born in 1867, was already in his early sixties when the decade began. He had been visiting the South of France regularly since 1909, and had settled there definitively in 1925, the year in which he married his long-time mistress Marie Boursin, known as Marthe. Marthe's difficult, reclusive character, and Bonnard's obsession with her, determined their style of life. Many of Bonnard's paintings from his South of France years show Marthe at her ablutions – she spent many hours a day in the bathroom. These canvases reveal Bonnard's ties to the immediate past, and some of these are surprising. The bathroom paintings suggest not only links with Renoir and Degas, both of whom tackled similar subject-matter, but also with the calm classicism of Pierre Puvis de Chavannes. The decorativeness of the treatment makes a piquant contrast with the voyeuristic intimacy of the subject-matter. Yet when we compare these late Bonnards to Puvis we are also

struck by the radicalism of the actual compositions. In Bonnard's *Nude in the Bath* (1935) in the Musée du Petit Palais the whole picture-plane is tilted towards us, to reveal the floating figure enclosed in her tub like an oyster in its shell.

Bonnard's gifts as a decorator also appear in a number of other works of this period, most notably in some large landscapes. The most ambitious were done in the late 1920s, and are notable for their deliberately unfocused quality, which carries the eye across the canvas instead of allowing it to concentrate on pictorial incidents somewhere near the centre. Here, too, one is conscious of a new and inventive way of looking clothed by an apparently conventional form. Bonnard would doubtless have done more commissioned work as a decorator, had it not been for the deteriorating economic situation. As it is, his decorations in the Palais de Chaillot in Paris, done in 1937, are a notable contribution to the revival of mural painting then taking place all over the world.

Another aspect of Bonnard's art is revealed by a series of late self-portraits. All have a haunted air. One of the strangest, a picture worthy of Edvard Munch, depicts the artist as a boxer, standing

62. Pierre Bonnard
Nude in the Bath, 1935

Oil on canvas
$36\frac{5}{8} \times 57\frac{13}{16}$in/93 × 147cm
Musée du Petit-Palais, Paris (Visual Arts Library)

63

63. Pierre Bonnard
Landscape in Normandy,
1926–29

Oil on canvas
24⅝ × 32in/62.5 × 81.5cm
Smith College Museum of Art
(Visual Arts Library)

bare-chested, with one fist raised in front of a mirror (1931). Despite the aggressiveness of the pose, the painting radiates a feeling of deep sadness. The unexpected style and mood of these self-portraits serve to reinforce a point made by Bonnard's later output as a whole – by that time he was a painter who had escaped from the confines of any specific movement or style, and who felt no particular compulsions to be either modern or unmodern.

This is not quite true of Matisse, only two years younger than Bonnard, and his neighbour and friendly rival. Matisse settled in the South almost a decade earlier than Bonnard, having lost the leadership of the Parisian avant-garde to Picasso. He did not, however, admit the permanence of the move, even to himself, until 1921, when he ceased living in temporary quarters in hotels. During the 1920s Matisse, painting a long series of sumptuous odalisques, had effected a reconciliation between himself and French bourgeois taste. By 1930, he was increasingly restless, and worried about his lack of contact with

64

the latest developments in Paris. He also had one eye fixed on Picasso's prodigious reputation. His first reaction was to make a break with an environment that had become stale and overfamiliar by going to Tahiti, which he had long wanted to see. He made the voyage via New York and San Francisco, laying up a stock of images he was to make full use of after World War II, but which made no swift appearance in his art. Later the same year he returned to the United States to sit on the jury of the Carnegie International Exhibition, and this trip was more immediately fruitful. He received an important commission to do a mural for the main hall of the Barnes Foundation at Merion, Pennsylvania in 1933. It was the sort of opportunity he had been subconsciously looking for, and something that because of its monumental nature, was in tune with the general artistic climate of the time. Rivera received major mural commissions in the United States at precisely the same period.

Matisse, of course, did not opt for the propagandistic subjects preferred by Rivera and his Mexican colleagues. The subject he chose was *The Dance*, a new version of a theme originally painted in 1910 for his Russian patron Shchukin. The area to be filled at Merion was a difficult one. It consisted of three lunettes, divided by two deep pendentives. Matisse's solution was to create a continuous composition, where the pendentives actually obscure parts of the figures.

66

The Barnes mural, which actually had to be painted twice because the artist had been given incorrect measurements, had the cathartic effect the artist must have hoped for. The forms are deliberately simple and severe, in this case for the practical reason that they had to harmonize with the scale and setting. Matisse said:

The expression of this painting should be associated with the severity of a volume of whitewashed stone, and an equally white, bare vault. Further, the spectator should not be arrested by this human character with which he would identify, and which by stopping him there would keep him apart from the great harmonious, living and animated association of the architecture and the painting.

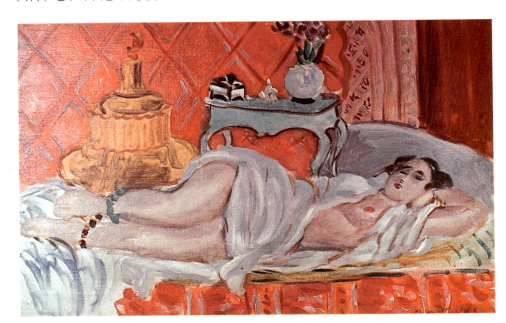

64. Henri Matisse
Odalisques, Red Harmony,
1926

Oil on canvas
14$\frac{15}{16}$ × 21$\frac{5}{8}$in/38 × 55cm
Private Collection

65

Nevertheless, the new style Matisse evolved for the specific needs of the Barnes commission came to pervade his art in general. He became involved in an increasingly stringent search for boldly drawn shapes. A picture often went through many stages, growing simpler and in a sense more rigid as it proceeded. A case in point is the celebrated *Pink Nude* (1935) in the Cone Collection in the Baltimore Museum of Art. This takes a theme associated with Ingres – the reclining odalisque – and rehandles it with tremendous boldness. Though Matisse's work continued to be colourful, paintings such as this one cannot be described as warm. Their rather chilly, consciously stylish classicism links them to what was happening to the French decorative arts at the same period, in the aftermath of Art Deco. It is one of the striking things about Matisse that he was able to take the not very distinguished bourgeois taste of the epoch, and transfer it on to the plane of high art. As with Bonnard, there are few, if any, direct intimations that Matisse was preoccupied with the deteriorating political situation. The two artists remained firmly locked away in paradises of their own creation. This withdrawal enabled them to create some of the finest art of the decade, just as characteristic in its way as the more political painting being done elsewhere. Characteristic because it demonstrates the degree to which the duty of being 'modern' was now subject to purely individual interpretation, even on the part of artists who remained intimately associated with the progress of the Modern Movement.

Not all the senior Modernists were as fortunate as Matisse during the 1930s. His fellow Fauve André Derain enjoyed an immensely high

reputation at the same epoch, but unlike Matisse's this has not been durable. Derain had begun to be bothered by the continuing gap between public taste and the ideals the Modernists had professed. In an interview with André Breton, the pope of the Surrealist Movement, he said:

> It's not the artist's role to educate the people; the people must educate him. It is the people who create words, give them their flesh, but the poet finds the rhythm. The greatest threat to art is too much culture. The true artist is an uncultivated man. The day when culture will become general, we will no longer need art. We will never find any consolation. But human beings are not capable of perfection and, above all, the artist must decline to make a sorry spectacle of himself – as a man who is resigned to acceptance.

Despite the ambiguity of the final phrase, Derain did resign himself to acceptance during the inter-war period. Where Matisse's classicism

65. Henri Matisse
Pink Nude 1935

Oil on canvas
26 × 36½in/66 × 92cm
Cone Collection, Baltimore
Museum of Art (Visual Art Library)

113

was bracingly rigorous, Derain opted for a more traditional version of
the Grand Manner, with reminiscences of nineteenth-century masters
such as Corot and Courbet. By 1931 occasional criticism was beginning
to be voiced. The veteran portraitist Jacques-Émile Blanche, no friend
of the avant-garde in principle, had some pertinent things to say:

> The faith and brio which marked his earlier works seem to have
> been replaced by the indifference of a sceptic weighed down by the
> number of masterpieces he has seen in museums and collections. His
> nudes and the series of heads still show intelligence and a painter's
> touch; poetry is still sometimes present, but it smells of fatigue.
> Youth has departed and what remains is a highly cerebral and rather
> mechanical art.

Derain's increasingly conservative views on art extended to politics as
well. During the war years he was lured into making a visit to
Germany, under official Nazi auspices, which did immense damage to
his reputation after the war.

Another, more personal and therefore more successful kind of
conservatism characterizes the art of Georges Braque. Braque had
been severely wounded during the war, and his absence on active
service, plus the long period of convalescence which followed when he
was invalided out of the French army, served to distance him from the
Parisian avant-garde. He did, however, have a solid foundation to build
on – everything which he and Picasso had created together in the
heroic Cubist years. Braque's solution was to try and reconcile Cubism
with the long-standing French tradition of *belle peinture*, taking
Chardin in particular as his exemplar. The result was a series of
still lifes in modified Cubist style – sometimes relatively large and
ambitious, but sometimes modest paintings manufactured in an almost
artisanal way, making no pretensions to striking originality, but
offered as specimens of Braque's supreme gifts as a craftsman. Like
Matisse's odalisques, these smaller paintings found a ready welcome
and helped to establish Braque with the bourgeois public.

Braque also showed the impact of the classical revival that took place
in France during the inter-war period. During the 1920s he painted a

66. Henri Matisse
The Dance II, 1933

11¾ × 47ft/3.57 × 14.32m
The Barnes Foundation, Merion
Station, Pennsylvania

series of *Canéphores* or *Ceremonial Basket-Bearers* — nude women **68**
carrying baskets of fruit upon their heads. The heavily statuesque
figures are a compromise between Cubist elision of planes and the
standard formulations of classical art.

The series of still lifes continued into the 1930s, but with certain
modifications. Those of the mid-1930s are consciously decorative, full
of sharp jagged shapes reminiscent of similar shapes to be found in the
decorative arts, especially the printed textiles of the period. In 1938
the mood became more sombre, and Braque started work on a series
of *Vanitás* still lifes, using the traditional image of a skull, and on
occasion adding a cross and rosary. These were clearly a reaction to the
darkening political climate, but also an affirmation of the painter's
belief in traditional symbols as a means of communicating with his
audience.

Figure paintings and drawings represent another aspect of Braque's
art at this time. Some of the drawings were made in a new technique:
they were incised into plaster panels which the artist had first covered
in dark paint, so that the line appears in white. The inspiration for
these, and for Braque's drawing of the figure in general, seems to have
come from pre-classical Greek gems, and from incised Etruscan
mirrors. He also seems to have been interested in Greek vase painting
— not the red-figure designs that had fascinated his neo-classical
predecessors, but the very early pots of the Geometric period.
Braque's interest thus marched in step with and even a little ahead of
the 'learned' taste of the time, which was already turning away from
the classicism of the fifth century and beginning to explore the earlier
periods of Greek art.

Three major members of the École de Paris went further than this in
their willingness to comment on some of the issues of the day.
Significantly none of them were French by birth. Two were Catalans,
who almost inevitably became involved in the tragedy of the Spanish
Civil war. The third was a Russian Jew.

It may seem surprising to speak of Chagall as having been, at any
period of his life, a political artist. It is perhaps more nearly correct to
say that, thanks to his heritage, he could not avoid contact with some

71

of the more brutal issues of the time. Whereas his rivals, with the exception of Matisse, were content to stay at home, Chagall travelled restlessly throughout the decade. At the beginning of the 1930s, the great dealer Ambroise Vollard, already a patron of Chagall, commissioned him to illustrate the Bible. In 1931 he and his family visited Palestine and were received with much honour. The visit reinforced Chagall's sense of his own Jewishness, even though he felt no temptation to throw in his lot with the new settlers.

In 1935 Chagall revisited a more familiar part of his heritage. He and his wife were invited to Poland, as guests of the Jewish Institute of Vilna. Vilna lay within the Jewish Pale of Settlement, and was only two hundred miles from Vitebsk, where Chagall had been born. During their visit, the Chagalls also saw the Warsaw ghetto. It was a last glimmer of a culture about to be destroyed by the holocaust. Antisemitism was strong in Poland, and Chagall's sensitivity made it easy for him to descry at least a few of the horrors to come.

The result was an increasing output of paintings on tragic themes, the greatest of these being the *White Crucifixion* of 1938. The painting's imagery is both complex and unorthodox. The figure of Christ is explicitly Jewish. His loincloth is the fringed Jewish tallith or prayer shawl, the seven branched Menorah burns at his feet. In the background there are various incidents that make the artist's meaning plain – a Nazi brownshirt sets a synagogue on fire; weeping Jewish elders float in the air and replace the lamenting angels of medieval art. The most curious detail of all occurs near the upper left margin. A squad of soldiers waving red banners enters a burning village. Do they represent the Red Army rushing to the rescue? In the France of that period the Front Populaire was busy putting forward the idea that the Soviet Union was the only ally who could help check the Nazi menace.

The ironic thing is that Chagall did not wholly believe his own message. When the war came and the Germans invaded France, the painter and his family lingered dangerously long, convinced that he was now too famous to be molested. The Chagalls waited until they were stripped of the French nationality they had only recently acquired – after difficulties caused by Chagall's early involvement

67. André Derain
The Road, 1931

Oil on canvas
25 9/16 × 19 5/8 in/65 × 50cm
Musée Orangerie, Paris (Visual Arts Library)

68. Georges Braque
Canéphores, 1923

Musée National d'Art Moderne

with the Russian Revolution, which had brought him the office of commissar. In April 1941 they had moved to Marseilles, ready to make their departure. Here they were arrested during a raid on the hotel where they were staying, and only freed through the urgent intervention of Varian Frey, head of the Emergency Rescue Committee, and Harry Bingham, the American Consul General in Marseilles. On 7 May Marc and Bella Chagall crossed the Spanish border on their way to the United States. Many European refugee artists had already preceded them.

Though the *White Crucifixion* is an exception in Chagall's work, it is nevertheless fully integrated within the general range of the artist's style. One cannot quite say this about the 'political' sculptures of Julio González, which are in quite a different idiom from the bulk of his

mature work. It must be said, however, that González took an exceptionally long time to reach artistic maturity. Born in 1876, he only became a complete and original artistic personality in the 1930s. His beginnings were in a family metalsmiths' shop in Barcelona, and his original ambition was to be a painter. This ambition was shared by his brother Joan, and the two of them left their native city in Picasso's wake and came to Paris around 1900. Here success eluded them. Joan, the older and more outgoing of the two brothers, died in 1908. Julio felt the blow deeply and suffered profoundly from melancholia for many years. By the mid-1920s he had turned to sculpture, but this was eclectic in style and small in scale. The decisive impulse came when Picasso, who had known González since their Barcelona days, summoned him to give technical assistance with new iron constructions.

69. Georges Braque
The Duet, 1937

Oil on canvas
130 × 160cm
National Museum of Modern Art,
Paris (Visual Arts Library)

González suddenly began to make elegant iron sculptures of his own. His ambition, as he said, was 'to draw in space'.

Though the debt to Picasso remains evident in González's work, the linear sculptures he produced are notable for their quirkiness and wit. They have had a profound influence on more recent work – David Smith, in particular, owed a great deal to them, and Smith is perhaps the central figure in post-war sculpture as a whole. But there is also another and quite different group of sculptures. Most of these were inspired by the conflict in Spain, and the image González uses to symbolize war-torn Catalonia is that of Montserrat – the Catalonian holy mountain personified as a Spanish peasant woman. Her most complete embodiment is an overlifesize statue made in 1936–7, which shows her standing with a sickle in her hand and a child on her arm. This was created for the Spanish Pavilion at the Paris Exposition Universelle of 1937. Like the majority of González's mature sculptures it is made of wrought iron, but the sculptor here abandons his technique of drawing in space to produce a solidly three-dimensional image, not unlike the heroic sculptures being made in Russia at the same period.

The most complex and instructive artistic career in the France of the 1930s was that of Picasso himself. Here private and public themes mingle in an especially intricate way, with the public ones becoming more prominent as the political horizon grew darker. Their expression has a directness and sometimes a brutality peculiar to the artist. Of all the great masters of Modernism Picasso was the one who remained most intimately in touch with a world of inner feeling. Increasing age and increasing celebrity made no difference.

The tone of the first years of the decade was largely set by Picasso's deteriorating marriage with the Russian dancer Olga Koklova, and his liaison with a young Swiss girl, Marie-Thérèse Walter. The dark side of his situation was expressed in a number of striking paintings. One is the *Crucifixion* which he painted early in 1930. It makes an astonishing contrast with Chagall's *Crucifixion* of eight years later. Where the meaning of Chagall's version is public, that of Picasso's is almost entirely private. The painting has no tenderness – it is an outcry of rage

72

70. Georges Braque
Blue and Red Guitar or the Bottle of Marc, 1930

Oil on canvas
51⅛ × 29⅛in/130 × 74cm
Private Collection (Visual Arts Library)

71. Marc Chagall
White Crucifixion, 1938

Oil on canvas
61 × 55in/155 × 139.5cm

The Art Institute of Chicago (Visual
Arts Library)

and pain. One especially significant detail is the draped head with gnashing jaws superimposed on Christ's breast. At about the same period Picasso was producing a series of terrifying female images – one of the best known is the *Seated Bather* (early 1930s) in the Museum of Modern Art, New York, where the figure has been aptly compared to a praying mantis.

The hostility towards women that seems to manifest itself here is contradicted by the works connected with Picasso's liaison with Marie-Thérèse. There are tranquil nudes, lyrical poems of praise to the wonders of the female body. There is also a series of large sculptured heads for which she was the model. One of the things that fascinated Picasso about Marie-Thérèse was her powerful profile, and this is an aspect of her appearance he stresses. Yet it is a clue to the essentially metaphorical nature of his imagination that in some cases he transforms her nose and cheek-bones into forms that suggest the male genitalia.

The chaos of Picasso's private life at this time makes an ironic contrast with the upward surge of his public reputation. In 1932 he held his first major retrospective exhibition at the Galerie Georges Petit in Paris. Up to that moment Picasso's work had been more talked about than seen. Large tracts of his production had remained unknown to the general public. His retrospective exhibition established him firmly as one of the two or three most important artists of the twentieth century.

Picasso was not content to rest on his laurels, though his biographers have noted a falling off in his production of paintings during the mid-1930s. The missing paintings were to some extent replaced by a large production of graphic work. During 1933 Picasso created some of his best-known etchings, on the theme of *The Sculptor's Studio*. In a new and lighter version of the classical style he had used in the early 1920s these show a bearded sculptor's artistic and amorous involvement with a beautiful young model. Picasso had tackled versions of this theme before, and it was especially apt, given his current involvement with Marie-Thérèse, which replicated the story in real life. But he also introduced a new element – the presence of the brutish, bull-headed

72. Julio González
Le Montserrat, 1936–7

Wrought and welded iron
64$\frac{15}{16}$ × 18$\frac{1}{2}$ × 18$\frac{1}{2}$in/165 × 47 × 47cm
Collection Stedelijk Museum,
Amsterdam

Minotaur. The Minotaur sometimes appears as a third party as the lovers revel. There are also hints of something darker. One print in the series shows the Minotaur dying in an arena, the victim of a young hero who kneels above him.

Later the mood is unambiguously tragic, though many ambiguities remain elsewhere. In a series of prints done in 1934–5 Picasso once again featured the Minotaur. In one image he is blind and supports himself with a stick. He is led by a little girl holding a dove, while watching fishermen shrink from him in terror. Here two myths seem to have been conflated – that of the Minotaur and that of Oedipus. It is worth remembering that Oedipus, though tragic, is not innocent. He owes his blindness to crimes he was for long unconscious of having committed. Another of these prints is Picasso's largest etching. It **76** depicts a *Minotauromachia* (1935). In this scene the Minotaur is a wholly threatening figure – he advances inexorably into the picture space – a woman dressed as a matador has already been mortally wounded and tumbles from her horse, which is frantically trying to escape. Less agitated, a man climbs a ladder in order to get away. The only person who is unafraid is a young girl who holds out a bunch of flowers to halt the monster's advance.

Picasso's Minotaurs cannot be interpreted straightforwardly. In *The Sculptor's Studio* the half-man, half-beast is chiefly an *alter ego*, an emanation of man's animal nature, and therefore of an aspect of Picasso himself. In the prints done in 1935 the Minotaur seems to symbolize something far more complex. Simultaneously pitiable and menacing, he is an emblem of humanity revealed in all its grossness and the herald of the horrors now slowly lifting themselves above the European horizon. Picasso's unconscious mind clearly sensed what lay in store.

By 1936 Picasso had a new personal entanglement, with Dora Maar, a more intelligent and also a far more complex woman than Marie-Thérèse Walter. Their relationship seems always to have been difficult, and Picasso immortalized Dora, not as a tranquil moon-**77** goddess, as he did in the case of her rival, but as *The Weeping Woman* whom he portrayed a number of times in the following year. Yet one cannot take it for granted that Dora weeps for purely private reasons.

The Spanish Civil War had now broken out, and for her as for Picasso the Catalan this was a cataclysmic event. Picasso was in closer touch with Spain than he had been for some years. In 1936 a group of young admirers had arranged a show for him in Barcelona – the first exhibition of his work to be held in Spain since 1902.

Picasso's first gesture of sympathy for the Republican cause was to produce *The Dream and Lie of Franco* (1937), a folder with two etchings divided into nine scenes which contained a facsimile of a poem by the artist attacking Franco in violent terms. The form chosen was deliberately popular – the nine scenes function like successive frames in a strip cartoon. The imagery has the violence of Goya's *Los Desastres de la Guerra* (1808–14), which must inevitably have been in Picasso's mind.

The artist's major contribution to the Republican side (he made several pecuniary ones) was not however *The Dream and Lie of Franco*

73. Pablo Picasso
Crucifixion, 1930

Oil on wood
$19\frac{5}{8} \times 25\frac{3}{4}$in/50 × 65.5cm
Musée Picasso, Paris (Visual Arts Library)

78

74. Pablo Picasso
Bust of a Woman, 1932

Bronze
24⅜ × 10³⁄₁₆ × 14¹⁵⁄₁₆in/62 × 26 × 38cm
Musée Picasso, Paris (Visual Arts
Library)

but the huge painting *Guernica*. This is on a scale that allows us to count **2** Picasso, as well, among the ranks of the muralists. The painting at the same time condemns and commemorates the destruction of the Basque capital by bombing in April 1937, which resulted in the loss of many lives.

Despite its topical subject, and the need to get it finished in time for a specific occasion, *Guernica* was planned with meticulous care. The composition underwent substantial changes before it was completed. These were documented by the vigilant camera of Dora Maar, who was a professional photographer. Many of the images the painting contains had appeared previously in Picasso's work. In particular there are echoes of the Minotaur series – chief among them the shrieking horse, and the bull which seems like a surrogate for the Minotaur himself. The screaming woman in the centre is not a descendant but a progenitor – she precedes the *Weeping Women*, which were painted immediately afterwards. *Guernica* generated new images for Picasso as well as employing existing material.

In creating the picture, he made no compromises with Modernism in order to reach a wide audience – differing in this respect from nearly all the other muralists of the 1930s with the exception of Matisse. Picasso assumed that the intensity of his personal vocabulary of images would enable his picture to speak for itself. The greatness of his achievement was that he managed to link these intensely private images together in such a way that they made a coherent statement about a public event. Picasso was the first to admit that *Guernica*, because it was openly propagandistic, was an exception in his work. He even admitted that it was possible in this case to assign specific allegorical meanings to some of the symbols. Cross-questioned on the subject by a rather naïve young American soldier in the period immediately following the Liberation (a time when he was probably more open to such approaches than he was at any other), Picasso said: 'The bull here represents brutality, the horse the people.' In May 1937, when he was still working on the painting, he made a public declaration about it which was almost as explicit: 'In the panel on which I am working and which I call *Guernica*, and in all my recent

75. Pablo Picasso
The Sculptor's Studio, 1933

Etching
7⅝ × 10½in/19.3 × 26.6cm
Collection of the Abby Aldrich
Rockefeller Print Room, The
Museum of Modern Art

works of art, I clearly express my abhorrence of the military caste which has sunk Spain in an ocean of pain and death . . .'

Other, less specifically political paintings represent Picasso's reactions to the gloomy news of the day. He began a series, continued during the war, showing a cockerel with its legs tied about to be slaughtered by a little girl – the cockerel is significant both as the symbol of male virility and as the national emblem of France. Picasso also did paintings of a cat tormenting a bird. One, dated April 1939, shows the creature with a brutishly human face. Yet Picasso was not entirely preoccupied by thoughts of this kind. His last major canvas to be completed before the war, *Night Fishing at Antibes* (1939), shows a timeless Mediterranean ritual – the spearing of fish attracted to the boat by acetylene flares.

Of all the artists whose work has been discussed here, Picasso was the one who reacted most directly to the pressure of outside events. His uniqueness is to be found in the fact that he was without

hierarchies. For him a new love affair and a horrifying public event like
the bombing of Guernica were both equally legitimate as subjects.
They were also things to be treated on precisely the same footing,
because each caused a seismic shock within the psyche that had to find
expression in art.

The established artists of his own generation who were French by
birth did not react in the same direct way. There were a number of
reasons for this. The first was the traditional French search for
harmony and order, which survived the Modernist explosion, and
which is particularly marked in both Matisse and Braque. In a more
particular and specific sense the first masters of Modernism in France
still had their roots in the doctrine of 'art for art's sake' espoused by
their Symbolist predecessors. Their whole instinct was to stand aside
from public events. Elsewhere matters had been different. In Italy and
in Russia, for example, the pioneering Modernists soon found themselves involved in politics. One of the ways in which Marinetti, the

76. Pablo Picasso
Minotauromachia, 1935

Etching printed in black
$19\frac{1}{2} \times 27\frac{7}{16}$in/49.5 × 70cm
The Museum of Modern Art, New
York. Purchase Fund

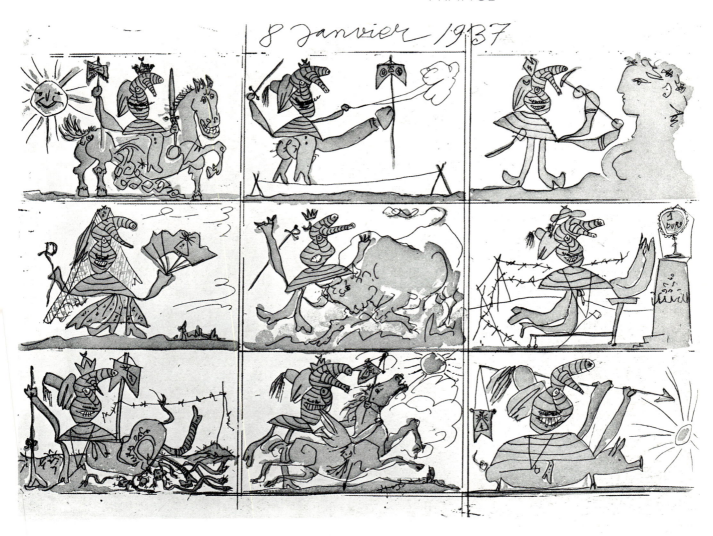

8 Janvier 1937

leader of the Italian Futurists, differed most sharply from his French contemporaries was in his conviction that art was, by its very nature, a political weapon. The Russian Constructivists, many of them influenced by Marinetti at their beginnings, agreed.

Yet, in an ironic and negative sense, there is after all something political about the directions taken by Matisse and Braque, Bonnard and Derain, during an increasingly turbulent decade. It is as if they were trying to use their art to erect a barrier against the ever-increasing pressure of events.

78. Pablo Picasso
The Dream and Lie of Franco

Etching and aquatint
$12\frac{3}{8} \times 16\frac{9}{16}$in/31.4 × 42cm
The Museum of Modern Art, New York. Gift of Mrs Stanley Resor

77. Pablo Picasso
The Weeping Woman, 1937

Oil on canvas
$23\frac{1}{2} \times 19\frac{1}{4}$in/60 × 49cm
Private Collection (The Bridgeman Art Library)

Parisian Fashions: Surrealism and Neo-Classicism

From its beginnings, modern art in France had been dependent for its existence on a small group of enlightened private patrons. This situation did not change during the 1930s. Indeed, thanks to the worldwide economic depression, the circle of patronage narrowed. Artists competed to attract the attention of a small group of wealthy people, often intelligent and enlightened, but also fickle and capricious. It is always hard, once a specific moment has passed, to define a climate of taste. One way of attempting it, slightly crude perhaps, but at the same time practical, is to look at the impact made by the fine arts on the frivolous world of fashion. If one wants to gauge the fluctuations of taste in the Paris of the 1930s, there is probably no surer guide than the enthusiasms of Elsa Schiaparelli. Schiaparelli was universally acknowledged to be the most innovative couturier of the time. She kept closely in touch with the world of avant-garde artists. It is possible to trace a clear line of development in the collections she designed during the course of the decade.

Schiaparelli's career as a Paris dress designer started in 1927. To begin with she specialized in sweaters and clothes 'pour le sport'. By 1930 she was already recognized as an important new force in fashion — her clothes in that year made use of grid-patterned fabrics that reflected the influence of Mondrian. But she did not remain faithful to 'purist' tenets for long. Soon she was in full pursuit of the Surrealists. Her new salon in the Place Vendôme was furnished with objects designed by the sculptor Alberto Giacometti and his brother; and many details of her outfits, but especially her hats, jewellery, and buttons were inspired by Salvador Dali. One of her more sensational creations was a hat in the form of a giant shoe, another was a handbag shaped like a telephone. Dali himself designed ceramic buttons for her which represented a fly perched on a piece of chocolate; there were also buttons, made to look like sweets, dice, and typewriter keys. Only towards the very end of the 1930s did Surrealist influence over Schiaparelli start to recede. In the winter of 1936–7 she launched a 'Neo-classical' collection, and this was followed by a 'Cosmic' collection in the winter of 1938–9. This latter, with its lavish use of astrological signs, demonstrates the impact made on Schiaparelli by

79

79. Christian Bérard
*Three evening dresses by
Madame Schiaparelli*, 1938

Union Française des Arts du
Costume, Paris (Visual Arts
Library)

the work of the painter and stage-designer Pavel Tchelitchew; and it is
perhaps no accident that fashion drawings of the collection were made
by Christian 'Bébé' Bérard, Tchelitchew's colleague and rival. Bérard
was more accessible to Schiaparelli because Tchelitchew himself had
already departed for America.

The strong influence of Surrealist painting on high fashion was ironic
because the Surrealist Movement professed principles that were
extremely hostile to those of the world of *haute couture*. Despite its
strong identification with the world of the visual arts, Surrealism had
begun as something primarily intellectual and literary. Its formidable
'pope' and organizer, the writer André Breton, believed that it should
be identified with the forces of political revolution, which in his mind
meant with Russian Communism. On the other hand, he did not wish
to put the movement under the control of the Communist Party. The
conflict between two authoritarian outlooks created almost unbear-
able tensions for his followers, and soon triggered a series of rows and

expulsions. For many Surrealists the attractions of orthodox Communism in the end proved irresistible. A major row broke out in 1930 when one of the leading figures in the movement, the poet Louis Aragon, participated in the Second International Congress of Revolutionary Writers which was held in Kharkov under Soviet auspices. Aragon departed for Russia with many promises to uphold the Surrealist viewpoint. He returned a convinced Communist and almost immediately published a violent poem, *Front Rouge*, which called for the murder of French political leaders and the killing of the 'trained bears of social democracy'. The government prosecuted him for incitement to murder. Breton disliked the poem but was not yet ready to break with his headstrong disciple. He defended *Front Rouge* on the grounds that Aragon didn't really mean what he said:

> We protest against this attempt to interpret a poetic text for judiciary ends, and demand an immediate cessation of the prosecution.

Aragon was not unnaturally offended by this means of defence, and also saw a useful chance of martyrdom vanishing. He in turn disavowed Breton. The resultant breach between orthodox Communism and Surrealism was never truly healed – the quarrel between Aragon and Breton came to seem symbolic of the general hardening of positions which took place in France during the decade.

This hardening did not affect painters as much as it did writers. There were several reasons for this. An obvious one was painting's position as a non-verbal art. Another was more practical – the majority of the leading Surrealist artists were not French, and had good reasons not to commit themselves fully to political action that might draw hostile attention from the French authorities.

Max Ernst was German, born in Cologne in 1891. He very early formed links with the German Dadaists, and his work attracted Breton's attention in 1920, four years before the First Surrealist Manifesto was issued. Breton advised the young artist to exhibit in Paris, and this Ernst did, but, because of visa difficulties, he was only able to move to France himself in 1922. Once there, he decided that he

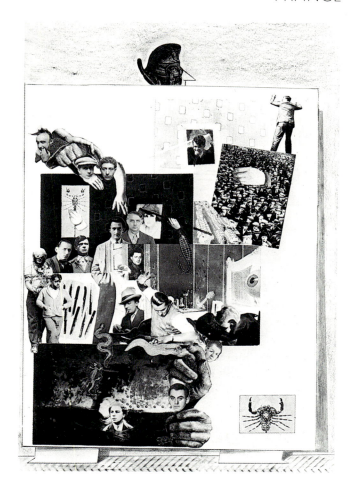

80. Max Ernst
Loplop Introduces Members of the Surrealist Group, 1931

Cut-and-pasted photographs, and pencil frottage
$19\frac{3}{4} \times 13\frac{1}{4}$in/50.1 × 33.6cm
The Museum of Modern Art, New York. Purchase

80

had had enough of Germany, and that his own future lay in the French art-world. By 1930 he was a mature artist, widely respected for the invention of a new form of collage. He used the technique not, as the Cubists did, in order to introduce something raw and unedited into designs where reality was otherwise intricately re-synthesized after being resolved into very basic elements, but as a way of producing a collision of incongruous images. Despite Breton's support and patronage Ernst did not believe in the orthodox Surrealist doctrine of 'pure psychic automatism'. He thought of the work of art as a found object, dredged in the crude state from the depths of the unconscious mind, but afterwards perfected and polished so as to bring out its true meaning and character.

Collage was only one of the techniques Ernst used for generating new images. Others were frottage (a rubbing made from a piece of wood or other small item); grattage (where successive layers of paint were scratched from a surface); and decalcomania (where thinned paint was pressed on to the canvas using a smooth-faced object, such as

135

81. Max Ernst
The Entire City, 1935–6

Oil on canvas
23½ × 32in/58 × 80cm
Kunsthaus, Zurich (Visual Arts
Library)

a pane of glass). The forms Ernst obtained by using these techniques were painstakingly elaborated, and the finished results demonstrated his kinship with the great German artists of the past, in particular with the leading Romantic Caspar David Friedrich, and with Albrecht Altdorfer of the sixteenth-century Danube School.

The way in which Ernst elaborated his found material was naturally affected by his state of mind at the time. He projected his own preoccupations into these random marks and splashes and smears of paint. As early as the mid-1920s his pictures began to echo his anxieties about the course of events in Europe. In 1925 Hitler's *Mein Kampf* was published. In 1927 Ernst produced several paintings on the theme of *The Horde*, which represented the nightmarish advance of an array of monsters. In the 1930s he returned more insistently to this theme, and both the images and the titles of the paintings became more specific. One group done in 1935 and closely related to *The Horde* is collectively entitled *Barbarians Moving Westwards*. It does not take much guessing to discover who the 'barbarians' are. Related to this group is another, whose sarcastic titles mock the euphemisms employed by totalitarian

rulers. One painting is called *Confidences*, another, especially gloomy and threatening, is *The Triumph of Love*. At this period there are also paintings of cities (*The Entire City*; *Petrified City*) which seem to prophesy the fate of Europe's historic towns when exposed to total war. Most violent and frightening of all are three paintings done in 1937, each of which is called *The Angel of Hearth and Home*. Ernst, usually reluctant to attach specific meanings to his art, admitted that these made direct reference to the fate of the Republicans in Spain:

> This is of course an ironic title for a kind of juggernaut which crushes and destroys all that comes in its path. That was my impression at the time of what would probably happen in the world, and I was right.

When the catastrophe came, Ernst was extremely lucky to escape from Europe with his life. In 1939, the French authorities imprisoned him as an enemy alien. He was freed thanks to representations made by the French Surrealist poet Paul Éluard, but was re-arrested when the Germans arrived in May 1940. After one unsuccessful attempt at escape, he finally managed to get away, with the Gestapo hot on his track, and emigrated via Spain to New York, where he joined other members of the Surrealist group. The painting that summarizes his feelings about what he was leaving behind him is the large *Europe after the Rain* (1940–42), begun in France and finished in America. This has since become an inspiration to numerous illustrators of science fiction and shows a universe transformed and depopulated by some melancholy catastrophe.

The more closely one examines the body of Ernst's work done in the 1930s, the less purely personal it seems. An unexpectedly high proportion consists of pictures that are political metaphors.

82. Max Ernst
Europe after the Rain, 1940–2

Oil on canvas
$21\frac{1}{2} \times 58\frac{1}{2}$in/54.5 × 145.5cm
Hartfield USA, Wadsworth Atheneum (Visual Arts Library)

82

More unexpectedly, there is also a strongly political element in the paintings made during the 1930s by Salvador Dali. Dali was not one of the original Surrealist group, but a brilliant late recruit. At one stage Breton counted on him to make up for the defection of former comrades such as Aragon, though he was soon to be disappointed. A member of the lively avant-garde which continued to flourish in Catalonia even after Picasso's departure for Paris, Dali first impressed Breton and the group surrounding him thanks to his extraordinary

83 short film *Un Chien Andalou*, made in collaboration with Luis Buñuel, and premiered in Paris in 1929, where it created a resounding scandal. For some time Dali had been painting under the influence of first generation Surrealists such as Jean Arp, Yves Tanguy and Joan Miró, and the film paved the way for him to join the group. In November 1929 Dali held his first one-man show in Paris, and Breton wrote the preface to the catalogue. Both Breton and Éluard bought paintings, but

84 the chief item, *Dismal Sport* (1929), much noticed because of certain scatological details, was bought by the Vicomte de Noailles, perhaps the most important patron of modern art in France. He hung it in his dining-room, between a Cranach and a Watteau. Dali had 'arrived'.

The paintings Dali showed in 1929 were a working out of his personal obsessions in the light of Freudian theory, and in particular that of Freud's classic text on the *Interpretation of Dreams*. The meticulous technique deliberately recalled the Salon painting of the nineteenth century – Dali professed a great admiration for Meissonier. The work thus combined images guaranteed to shock the conventional bourgeoisie and stylistic features calculated to make the avant-garde feel extremely uneasy. But this was not enough to satisfy the painter. He wanted to offend his closest allies as well. In 1933 he painted the

85 *Enigma of William Tell*, an allegory of his own relationship to his father, who is shown with Lenin's face, holding the infant Dali in his arms. On the child's head, in place of the apple required by the Tell legend, is a raw cutlet, which hints that the father has cannibalistic intentions, and is preparing to eat his infant. The main figure's right buttock is enormously elongated, so that it suggests a giant, flaccid penis. Its flaccidity is emphasized by the fact that it is supported with a crutch.

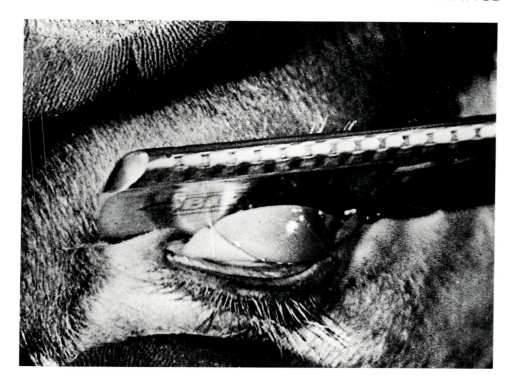

83. Salvador Dali and Luis Bunuel
Un Chien Andalou, 1928
Edimedia, Paris

The *Enigma of William Tell* was the more offensive to Breton because it was timed to coincide with the Aragon affair. Early in 1934, as a result of this and other misdemeanours, Dali was summoned to appear before a kind of Surrealist tribunal, held at Breton's flat. Judgment had already been passed before the culprit appeared: 'Dali having been found guilty on several occasions of counter-revolutionary actions involving the glorification of Hitlerian fascism, the undersigned propose ... that he be excluded from Surrealism as a fascist element and combated by all available means.'

When Dali appeared the proceedings were farcical. The artist was running a fever (so he claimed), and was bundled up in layers of sweaters, which he gradually removed. He had a thermometer in his mouth, which he took out from time to time to consult while Breton was berating him. On the other hand, he did not take it out when his own turn came to speak, and it muffled his replies – though these were to the point. Dali said that the accusations against him were based on 'political and moral criteria which did not signify in relation to (his) paranoiac-critical concepts'. Addressing himself directly to his chief accuser, he added: 'So, André Breton, if tonight I dream I am screwing you, tomorrow morning I will paint all our best fucking positions in the greatest wealth of detail.' Breton had a horror of homosexuality, and this was a piece of deliberate provocation. But eventually Dali knelt down before the group and swore to give up his ideas on fascism.

139

He also solemnly confirmed that he was not an enemy of the proletariat.

The reconciliation did not last. In Dali's mind both Hitler and Lenin were contemporary phenomena, and had become part of his repertoire of 'delirious dream subjects':

> I often dreamed of Hitler as a woman (Dali wrote later, in his *Unspeakable Confessions*). His flesh, which I imagined whiter than white, ravished me ... There was no reason for me to stop telling one and all that to me Hitler embodied the perfect image of the great masochist who would unleash a world war solely for the pleasure of losing and burying himself beneath the rubble of an empire: the gratuitous act par excellence that should indeed have warranted the admiration of the surrealists ...

Unable to abandon the subject, in 1937 Dali painted a successor to the *Enigma of William Tell*, entitled the *Enigma of Hitler*. A scrap of a photograph of Hitler, painted in meticulous *trompe-l'œil*, lies in a dish under a deliquescent telephone. A ghostly umbrella hooked to a branch symbolizes the presence of Chamberlain, and the picture can be read as a comment on the negotiations that led to the Munich agreement.

For Dali, the *Enigma of Hitler* is an unusually thin work – thinly painted and without much power of suggestion. Far more powerful and memorable are two paintings that refer to the Spanish Civil War – *Soft Construction with Boiled Beans: Premonition of Civil War*, and *Autumn Cannibalism*. The first is a prophetic image preceding the outbreak of the war, which took place in July 1936, by several months. Dali has described it as follows:

86
87

> In this picture I showed a vast human body breaking out into monstrous excrescences of arms and legs tearing at one another in a delirium of auto-strangulation. As a background to this architecture of frenzied flesh devoured by a narcissistic and biological cataclysm. I painted a geological landscape, that had been uselessly revolutionized for thousands of years, congealed in its 'normal course'. The soft structure of that great mass of flesh in civil war I

84. Salvador Dali
Dismal Sport, 1929

Oil on canvas
Private Collection

141

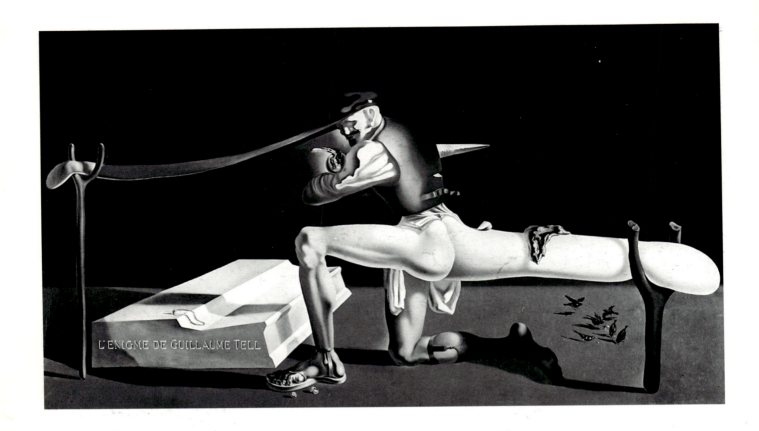

85. Salvador Dali
The Enigma of William Tell,
1933

Oil on canvas
79⁵⁄₁₆ × 136³⁄₈in/201.5 × 346.5cm
Museum of Modern Art, Stockholm

embellished with a few boiled beans, for one could not imagine swallowing all that unconscious meat without the presence (however uninspiring) of some mealy and melancholy vegetable.

Premonition of Civil War has reminded many viewers of Goya. The gigantic figure with its warring limbs is Goya's *Colossus* in a new guise, busily destroying himself, simultaneously victim and aggressor. Yet Goya, like Ernst, always resisted attempts to attach specifically political meanings to his art. Speaking of *Autumn Cannibalism*, painted after the war had begun, Dali commented:

> These Iberian beings, eating each other in autumn, express the pathos of the Civil War considered (by me) as a phenomenon of natural history as opposed to Picasso who considered it a political phenomenon.

Dali's art did him greater justice than some of the declarations he made at this epoch. Talking to Breton in February 1939 he said bluntly that: 'the contemporary world crisis was *racial* and that the solution to be applied should be a concerted effort by all people of white race to reduce all coloured people to slavery.' Breton naturally repeated this when announcing Dali's expulsion soon afterwards from the official Surrealist Movement. The breach made little or no difference to Dali's fortunes. He had been successfully courting the American rich and

142

86. Salvador Dali
Soft Construction with Boiled Beans: Premonition of Civil War, 1936

Oil on canvas
$39\frac{3}{8} \times 39$in/100×99cm
The Philadelphia Museum of Art:
The Louise and Walter Arensberg
Collection

87. Salvador Dali
Autumn Cannibalism, 1936

Oil on canvas
25$\frac{9}{16}$ × 25$\frac{9}{16}$in/65 × 65cm
The Tate Gallery, (& A.D.A.G.P.)
London

now spent more and more of his time in America. What his fellow-Surrealists found even more galling than his greed for money and his reactionary political views was the fact that he left the impression in the United States that he was the inventor of Surrealism, instead of being a comparative newcomer.

Dali's fellow-Catalan Joan Miró had a much longer-standing connection with the Surrealist group. He had been in touch with the Dadaists since 1917, and had met Francis Picabia when the latter came to Barcelona during World War I. Later, having gone to Paris, Miró immediately made contact with the founder members of the Surrealist group, and his own paintings were reproduced in the magazine *La Révolution surréaliste* as early as 1925. But he was notably silent when he attended Surrealist meetings and never committed himself without reserve to Surrealist doctrines.

His painting lay at the opposite extreme from Dali's. In place of Dali's academic precision, from the mid-1920s onwards Miró developed a language of cryptic and simplified signs. On occasion he used his

144

vocabulary to produce new versions of the masterpieces of the past, as if to stress both his own flexibility and the autonomy of the style that he had developed. One of his best-known pictures, the *Dutch Interior* of 1928 now in the Guggenheim Collection, Venice, is precisely what its title proclaims it to be. In fact it is a paraphrase of Jan Steen's *The Cat's Dancing Lesson* which Miró had seen in the Rijksmuseum, Amsterdam.

88

The beginning of the new decade found Miró emerging from a severe mid-life crisis. He was moderately successful. He had just, at the age of thirty-eight, married a girl from a family well-established in Majorca, thus reaffirming his links with his native Spain. Unlike Picasso, he remained a regular visitor, and spent every summer working at Montroig in Catalonia. His period of stock-taking was almost immediately followed by the Crash, and his output at the beginning of the 1930s was low because, like other artists, he had difficulty in selling his work. Nevertheless the mood of his painting at this period was serene. A second crisis came in 1935, when the images he produced suddenly became tense and violent. It was as if Miró sensed unconsciously that the political climate was becoming more threatening, and this mood was automatically echoed in his work. In 1935 and 1936 he produced two series of paintings whose subjects were nightmarish monsters. The first series was on cardboard, an ungrateful medium apparently chosen because of its crudity. *Personage in the Presence of Nature* (Philadelphia) shows a little hobgoblin being threatened by an enormous goat with a dragon's maw. The second series, either on copper or on masonite panels, is more carefully painted but equally violent in mood. A typical example is *Personages Attacked by the Form of a Mountain* (Baltimore). Here Miró's instinctive feeling that something nightmarish was about to happen in Spain was forcibly expressed.

89

Miró returned to France in the autumn of 1936, and did not set foot in Spain for the duration of the conflict. Throughout this period he rejected all attempts to make him discuss the Spanish political situation, though he did produce a mural (now lost) for the Spanish pavilion at the Paris Exposition Universelle of 1937, and also a striking poster, *Aidez l'Espagne*. His real reactions were expressed obliquely, through another shift in direction. He now seemed to want to protect

90

145

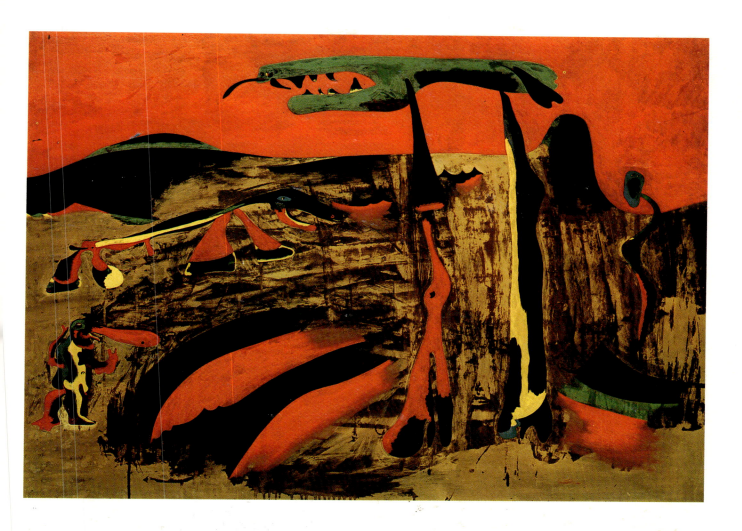

himself from the horrific phantasms that had invaded his work and returned unexpectedly to direct study of the model. He made numerous life-drawings at the famous *atelier libre*, La Grande Chaumière, and spent five months in 1937 painting the totally uncharacteristic *Still Life with an Old Shoe* (Museum of Modern Art, New York). This is composed of extremely humble, banal objects – a bottle, an apple with a fork stuck in it, the heel of a loaf of bread and the old shoe that gives the painting its title. Yet it is as much a portrait of tortured Spain as Picasso's *Guernica*. Everything the picture contains is transformed by an unearthly, hell-fire glow.

After he had purged himself of his feelings about Spain, Miró's work became tranquil again, despite the ever-worsening political situation. When the Germans made their breakthrough in May 1940, Miró was shut away at Varengeville in Normandy, painting the *Constellations*, which are among his most delightfully fanciful works. He made a difficult journey to Paris with his wife and daughter, then, despite the risk that he might not be well received by the Franco regime, took the first available train to Spain, eventually finding shelter with his wife's

89. Joan Miró
Personage in the Presence of Nature, 1935

Oil and gouache on board
29¾ × 42½in/75.5 × 108cm
Philadelphia Museum of Art: Louise and Walter Arensberg Collection

88. Joan Miró
Dutch Interior, 1928

Oil on canvas
36⁵⁄₁₆ × 28¹³⁄₁₆in/92.2 × 73.2cm
Peggy Guggenheim Collection, Venice; The Solomon R. Guggenheim Foundation

90. Joan Miró
Aidez L'Espagne, 1937

Poster
Lords Gallery

relations in Palma, where the *Constellations* were finished. Though he had given the Republicans public support, the new government did not make trouble for Miró, and he stayed in Spain till the end of the war.

Neither Dali nor Miró can be described as genuinely political artists, though clearly the political climate of the 1930s had a more direct effect on their art than is now generally admitted. The case is slightly different with André Masson who, of all the major Surrealist painters, was the slowest to win recognition. Yet Masson is also the artist who

148

comes closest to the method Breton prescribed – that of pure psychic automatism. He was overshadowed for two reasons – he was often at odds with the Surrealist junta; and he spent much time out of France.

Masson's violent temperament found an outlet at the beginning of the decade in a series of drawings of *Massacres*, which are prophetic in the sense that some of Dali's and Miró's work is also prophetic. Masson **91** tackled other, related themes at the same time – young girls wringing the necks of chickens, bull-fights and slaughterhouses. These he had in common with Picasso whom he sometimes anticipated rather than followed in his use of these images. Between 1934 and 1936 he lived in Spain, and the Civil War inspired him to make savage drawings that owe much to Goya – *Los Caprichos* as well as *Los Desastres de la Guerra*. These entitle him to be described as the most 'committed' of all the leading Surrealist artists. But the mood did not last. When Masson returned to France after the outbreak of the war, there was a period of recapitulation. The masterpiece of this time is *In the Tower of Sleep* (1938, Baltimore). This is in a broad sense philosophical rather than political – it shows mankind drowning in its own profusion of knowledge.

If Masson's work often reacts sensitively to the pressure of events, that of Yves Tanguy seems more or less immune to them. Tanguy was a self-taught artist, whose weird landscapes peopled with biomorphic forms exercised an important influence over the young Salvador Dali. Though these often suggest, like Ernst's *Europe after the Rain*, that some huge catastrophe has taken place, there is nothing to connect them specifically to outside events.

This is also the case with the sculptures made by Alberto Giacometti during his brief period as a Surrealist. These can communicate strong feelings of hostility (*Woman with Her Throat Cut*, 1932), threat (*Pointe à l'Oeil*) or alienation (*The Palace at 4 a.m.*, 1932–3), but they are personal **92** to Giacometti himself. In a statement made in 1933 he described his method of work:

For some years now I have only realized sculptures which have presented themselves to my mind in a finished state. I have

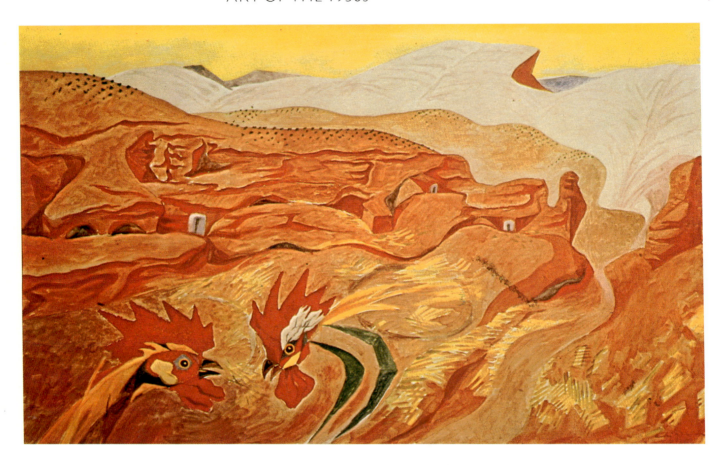

91. André Masson
Ibdes in Aragon, 1935

Oil on canvas
23⅝ × 36¾in/60 × 92.4cm
The Tate Gallery (& A.D.A.G.P.),
London

restricted myself to reproducing them in space without changing anything and without asking myself what they might signify (if I attempt to modify some part of one or if I have to search to get the scale, it's enough to make me lose myself completely, wreck the whole thing). Nothing has ever appeared to me in the form of a picture. I rarely see in the form of a drawing. The attempts I have sometimes embarked upon at consciously working out a picture – even a sculpture – have always failed. Once the sculpture is made I have a tendency to rediscover in it, transformed and displaced, images, impressions, facts which have profoundly moved me (often without my knowing it), forms which I feel are very close to me, although I am often incapable of identifying them, which always makes them more disturbing to me.

By the time this statement was made, Giacometti was already beginning his shift away from Surrealism, and between 1935 and 1940 he was working from models – a heresy for which he was expelled from the ranks of the Surrealists. If it had been possible for him to continue with his original method perhaps his work, too, would have shown

150

92. Alberto Giacometti
The Palace at 4 a.m., 1932–3

Construction in wood, glass, wire, string
$25 \times 28\frac{1}{4} \times 15\frac{3}{4}$ in/$63.5 \times 71.8 \times 40$cm
The Museum of Modern Art, New York. Purchase

signs of the stress and violence of those years. Surrealism, by putting the artist at the mercy of his unconscious, also laid him open to influences that could broadly be described as 'political'. The pressing anxieties of the time expressed themselves in this fashion through the work of leading Surrealist painters, and the external causes responsible for generating some of their most striking images are in many cases still recognizable.

Abstraction, Neo-Romanticism and Social Realism in France

Because Paris was universally regarded as the capital city of the visual arts during the 1930s, it attracted painters and sculptors from all over the world. As we have seen, the majority of the leading Surrealist painters were not French. Numerous other foreign artists settled in Paris, not because of political pressure, but because they regarded the city as the best place to live and work. One such was the Dutch painter, Piet Mondrian. Mondrian had spent a period in Paris before World War I, from December 1911 to July 1914. At this time he had come into contact with the Cubists. The war trapped him in his native Holland, and it was while he was waiting impatiently for it to end that he became one of the founders of *De Stijl*. Despite his dislike of the Dutch environment, contact with like-minded friends caused Mondrian's art to evolve very rapidly. The strictly ordered pure abstraction based on interlocking horizontals and verticals which Mondrian evolved during the war years, had almost reached its definitive form by the time he returned to Paris again in 1919. The final steps took place in the 1920s – Mondrian now used black lines on a white ground, sometimes alone, sometimes accompanied by rectangles in primary colours – red, yellow and blue. It was said at the time, and is sometimes said now, that once he had reached this point Mondrian made little or no further progress – that it was not until he arrived in the United States in 1940 that his art evolved once more, in response to the stimulus offered by New York.

It is true that this was the most sudden and dramatic change to take place in Mondrian's art for many years, but even in the Paris period a slow evolution is discernible. In the 1930s, for example, the characteristic black lines become more numerous and more closely spaced, so that sometimes they look like prison bars. If we admit what seems obvious – that the jagged rhythms of New York are interpreted in Mondrian's final masterpiece. *Broadway Boogie-Woogie* (1942–3), we might also be prepared to consider the idea that these oppressive paintings echo Mondrian's reaction to the deteriorating international situation. We know that he left Paris for London in 1938 because he already foresaw the coming conflict, and feared Paris would be bombed.

93. Fernand Léger
The Large Blue Cockerel, 1937

Oil on canvas
$51\frac{1}{2} \times 37\frac{3}{4}$in/130 × 96cm
Sotheby's

F. LÉGER
37

During Mondrian's long Paris period he lived very quietly, and was largely ignored by the kind of fashionable world that courted Dali. His most important sales were to visiting Americans, such as Katherine Dreier, who were aware of his importance as a pioneer of Modernism. Among artists, Mondrian was highly respected — most of all by the large group that concerned itself with abstract art. At the end of the 1920s, he formed a lasting friendship with the Uruguayan painter Joáquin Torres-García. He, Torres-García and the poet and critic Michel Seuphor had the idea of forming a group of abstract artists to resist the then-dominant Surrealist influence. They named it Cercle et Carré (Circle and Square), and it began to hold meetings in 1930. About eighty artists joined, and the response was such that a large exhibition was held in April 1930 at the Galerie 23. Among the artists included were Jean Arp, Willi Baumeister, Wassily Kandinsky, Le Corbusier, Fernand Léger, Piet Mondrian, Amédée Ozenfant, Antoine Pevsner, Kurt Schwitters, Henryk Stazewski, Jacques Stella, Sophie Taeuber-Arp, Joáquin Torres-García, Georges Vantongerloo and Friedrich Vordemberge-Gildewart. Despite this participation it was almost ignored by the Paris press, who were antagonized by the presence of such a high proportion of foreigners.

It was not until 1937 that this cosmopolitan school of abstract artists achieved any official recognition in France. In that year a survey exhibition was mounted in the Jeu de Paume, as a kind of footnote to the Paris Exposition Universelle. Called *Origines et développement de l'art international indépendant*, it was hurriedly put together as a substitute for a show of pictures from the Prado which had fallen **94** through. The moving spirit was Kandinsky, who was by this time living in France, having emigrated from Germany in 1933, but he could not be given any definite role because he was not a French citizen. The show attracted only 5,000 visitors, mostly from abroad, but even this was considered a triumph in the circumstances. Pure abstraction had never gained the foothold in France that it had achieved in Russia under the Constructivists or in Germany thanks to the Bauhaus.

Some distinguished artists lived out their lives in Paris without really participating in the busy Parisian art-world. One such was

Constantin Brancusi, who had arrived in Paris from his native Romania in 1904, and by 1908 had already begun to make his highly simplified direct carvings in stone and wood. By 1912 Brancusi had established his own distinctive style, which did not change radically for the rest of his life. He used and re-used a narrow range of themes, among them the *Bird in Space*, the *Cock Greeting the Sun*, and the *Endless Column*. In 1920 he ceased altogether to exhibit in Paris, after an incident when an attempt was made to exclude a work of his from the Salon des Artistes Indépendants on the grounds that it was indecent. One reason why he was able to do this was that he had found good patrons in America – more enthusiastic and willing to pay higher prices than those available to Mondrian. An exhibition held at the Brummer Gallery in New York in 1936 received tremendous publicity when the U.S. customs refused to grant Brancusi tax exemption for his sculptures, on the grounds that they were not works of art. The sculptor sued them for the return of duty paid and won.

Though Brancusi did not exhibit in Paris, and found few buyers there, he became an important legend. He lived simply in his studio in

94. Wassily Kandinsky
Dominant Curve, 1936

Oil on canvas
$50\frac{7}{8} \times 76\frac{1}{2}$in/129.2 × 194.3cm
Solomon R. Guggenheim Museum,
New York

the Impasse Ronsin, where he received a few friends. These distinguished visitors, who included Princess Murat, Jean Cocteau and Gertrude Stein, spread his reputation as one of the saints of art – the kind of creative genius that only the Parisian environment could sustain.

A friend of Brancusi's (they used to go to the music hall together), and almost equally isolated from the Paris art-world was the Russian-Jewish painter Chaïm Soutine. Soutine arrived in Paris eight years later than Brancusi, in 1912, and spent a long time in desperate poverty. He bore the marks of this all his life, though his fortune was made in 1923, when he attracted the attention of the wealthy American collector Albert C. Barnes, who bought almost the entire contents of his studio. In the 1930s Soutine had little to worry about materially. The decade brought him one-man shows in Chicago, New York and London, as well as a retrospective held in 1937 at the Musée du Petit-Palais in Paris – the kind of honour that came to few foreign artists in France at that time. His isolation was due to his own moody, eccentric and difficult character. The American writer Henry Miller, who at one time had the apartment above Soutine's and was friendly with him, described him as 'trying to recover from the wild life of other days'. His mistress, Gerda Groth, later spoke of him as 'a savage who fled from all worldliness'.

To look at Soutine's work is immediately to understand why he could have no school and belong to no formal grouping. He depends entirely on the spontaneity of his own feelings. It is these that simultaneously shape and deform the imagery he puts on canvas. The paintings of the 1930s are in general quieter and more tempered than those Soutine had produced earlier – this is clearly something that reflects the improvement in his own circumstances. The paintings of food, for example, continue to testify how very vivid his memories of hunger were. Soutine reacted almost entirely to basic stimuli of this kind: he was nothing if not self-centred. Broader issues escaped him. Though he was a stateless Jew, and thus more threatened than most by the deterioration of the international situation, anxieties of this sort are not reflected in the work of this profoundly anxious painter. There

95. Constantin Brancusi
Bird in Space, 1925

Polished bronze on marble and oak base
Bronze 49¾in/126.3cm high; sections 48⅛in/122.2cm high; (1 marble and 3 oak sections)
Philadelphia Museum of Art: Louise and Walter Arensberg Collection

is no trace of the foreboding one finds in the work of leading Surrealists, painted at the same period.

Soutine suffered the consequences of his inability to look outside his own immediate situation. At the last moment he tried to leave for America, where he had patrons and guarantors awaiting him, but he was unable to do so as he had long ago lost all his personal documents. When the Germans came, he was forced to register as a Jew, and led a restless, insecure life in remote country districts, where he hoped to escape attention. The uncertainty of his situation worsened the gastric ulcers from which he had long suffered. Brought clandestinely to Paris for an emergency operation, he died shortly after it had been performed, without regaining consciousness.

Unlike Mondrian and Brancusi, Soutine did find patrons in France, and was able to extract high prices from them. Chief among these patrons were the fashionable interior decorator Madeleine Castaing and her husband, who monopolized a large part of his production during the 1930s. What made his work acceptable, for all its roughness and wildness, was the fact that it was figurative, and many people in France – collectors, museum officials and critics – were consciously looking for a return to figurative art. It was an expectation shared by conservatives and left-wingers alike, but for different reasons: for the conservatives it corresponded to the much-wished-for *rappel à l'ordre*; for left-wingers it was in step with Soviet support for Socialist Realism.

In the fashionable world, the chief beneficiaries of this climate of taste were the Neo-Romantics. As we have already seen, they succeeded in distracting Schiaparelli from her interest in the Surrealists, but they have not survived the passage of time as successfully as Ernst, Miró and Dali. Only one artist connected with the group occupies a prominent position today, and even then art-historians often seem at a loss as to how to place him. This survivor is Balthus (the *nom de peintre* adopted by Balthasar Klossowski de Rola).

Born in Paris, Balthus was of Polish stock, but both his parents were German citizens. Thanks to World War I he spent an unsettled childhood divided between Germany and Switzerland. He owed his

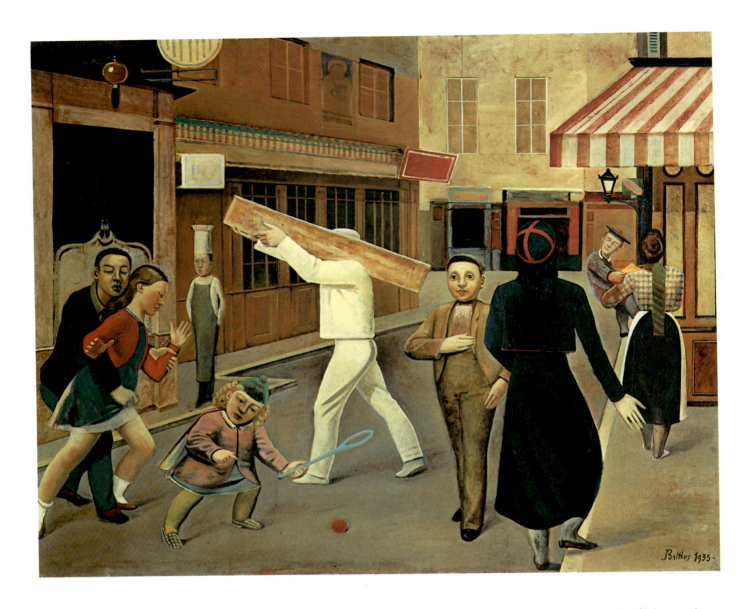

96. Balthus
The Street, 1933

Oil on canvas
6ft 4¾in × 7ft 10½in/195 × 240cm
Collection, The Museum of Modern
Art, New York. James Thrall Soby
Bequest

97. Balthus
André Derain, 1936

Oil on wood
44⅜ × 28½in/112.7 × 72.4cm
Collection, The Museum of Modern
Art, New York. Acquired through
the Lillie P. Bliss Bequest

start as an artist to the poet Rilke, who was a close friend of his mother.
Rilke arranged the publication of some illustrations to a children's
story done when Balthus was only eleven, and later had a hand in
introducing him to the art-world in Paris. The young painter was also
helped by André Gide. In the 1920s Balthus divided his time between
France and Italy. In Italy he made a special study of Piero della
Francesca, a master admired by his father, a professional painter who
became a well-known stage designer. In Paris he received advice from
established masters such as Bonnard.

Balthus's first exhibition was held in 1934 at the Galerie Pierre. It
caused a scandal almost as resounding as that aroused by Dali a few
years earlier. The show contained only a few large paintings, which
were a strange mixture of the stringently classical, the naïve and the
erotic. The most ambitious work, *The Street* (1933), still counts as one

158

98. Chaïm Soutine
Choir Boy, 1930

Oil on canvas
$25\frac{15}{16} \times 14\frac{1}{8}$ in/66 × 38cm
New York collection (J. Poses/
Visual Arts Library)

of the masterpieces of its period, though modern viewers do not see it in precisely its original form. The man embracing a young girl at the extreme left of the composition made a more explicitly sexual gesture until the work was altered to make it more acceptable to the Museum of Modern Art in New York. This small change hardly affects the composition as a whole and *The Street* is a good summary of the young Balthus's qualities. It is an extremely sophisticated picture, which draws on a wide range of sources, from crude popular prints (*imageries d'Épinal*) and illustrations to nineteenth-century children's books to Piero's *Flagellation* in the Palazzo Ducale at Urbino. It is almost as if Max Ernst had made certain small revisions to a painting by Seurat – *The Street* can be read as an urban companion piece to Seurat's *Baignade*.

A comparison with Ernst is in any case in order, since the strange uneasy atmosphere the pictures generate brings the Balthus of the period close to Surrealism. The difference is that there is nothing dislocated or openly 'fantastic' about Balthus's imagery – everything remains within the framework of the natural order.

Thanks to the stir created by his first exhibition, Balthus was able to make a career as a portrait painter. The list of his sitters shows that he was accepted within a world an artist like Mondrian was never able to penetrate, and where even Soutine remained an admired outsider. The majority of his subjects were fashionable women, among them the Vicomtesse de Noailles and the beautiful Lady Abdy. Balthus also painted two striking portraits of leading artists. One was of Miró, commissioned as a tribute by their mutual dealer; the other was of André Derain, who at this period had an important influence on Balthus's work. In addition to all this, Balthus followed in his father's footsteps as a stage designer. He was responsible for the sets and costumes for Antonin Artaud's production of Shelley's *The Cenci* (1935), an exemplification of Artaud's theories about a 'Theatre of Cruelty'.

97

Though Balthus built a big reputation among the cognoscenti, he was probably not as well known to the Paris art-world in general as Pavel Tchelitchew. Today the latter's reputation is not nearly as high as that of his one-time rival. Tchelitchew was a Russian émigré, who arrived penniless in Berlin in 1923, and quickly made a name as a designer for the stage. From Berlin, he soon transferred himself to Paris, and in 1928 Diaghilev employed him as the designer for the ballet *Ode*. His spectacular sets and lighting effects attracted a good deal of interest, though the piece was not a success. At the same time Gertrude Stein took Tchelitchew under her wing – a good beginning for any aspiring artist in the Paris of the time. Diaghilev was attracted to Tchelitchew partly because he was Russian, but also through his own instinct for what was going to be fashionable. Gertrude Stein may have been influenced not only by Tchelitchew's personal charm, but by the fact that he was reviving and rehandling ideas first used by Picasso in the Blue and Rose periods. Dependence on Picasso makes Tchelitchew's work look derivative now – he was one of the first artists to cannibalize the past of Modernism.

The same can be said of another artist who moved in the same circles and attracted a similar kind of patronage – Christian Bérard, who painted Cocteau and many members of his circle. Like Balthus and Tchelitchew, Bérard was involved with the stage, and stage design eventually became his principal occupation, to the detriment of his work as an easel painter.

Tchelitchew missed his chance in a different way. Rootless and restless, he spent increasing amounts of time in England during the early 1930s, partly because he had attracted the patronage of Edward James, the eccentric English millionaire who was also for a while one of the chief supporters of the Surrealists, and partly because he had formed a close connection with the poet Edith Sitwell. In 1936 he abandoned Europe and went off to make his fortune in America. Some of his most striking work was done in the late 1930s in New York – his portrait of Lincoln Kirstein, painted in 1937, is a particularly strong image. But neither Balthus nor Bérard was equipped to sustain the Neo-Romantic cause in France in quite the same fashion, and the movement, lacking both a champion and a real ideology (of the kind that Surrealism possessed) inevitably petered out and was forgotten after the war.

One figurative movement that did survive the war, but only briefly, was the French variety of Social Realism. Swept away by the rising tide of abstraction in the 1950s, those who belonged to it suffered almost total eclipse. Their work is now little known, scarcely available to the public, and in urgent need of re-examination, though a tentative start was made with the Pompidou Centre's exhibition 'Paris–Paris, 1937–1957' staged in 1981. Two leading artists in this group were André Fougeron and Boris Taslitzky. Much of their painting dealt directly with the political turmoil of the time, and the general style of their work was a mixture of realism and expressionism. Renato Guttuso was working in a similar manner in Italy.

A major artist who might have been expected to develop in the direction of Social Realism, and who failed to do so at this period, was Fernand Léger. Léger had moved from his own pre-war version of Cubism into Purism, which preoccupied him during the 1920s, though

99

100

99. Pavel Tchelitchew
Edith Sitwell, 1937

Oil on canvas
64 × 38in/162.5 × 96.5cm
Edward James Foundation

100. André Fougeron
Composition, 1946

(Artephot/Takase)

some paintings of this epoch, notably *Le Mécanicien*, painted at the very beginning of the decade, do testify directly to his sympathy with the proletariat. More frequently the imagery of this period expresses his excited admiration for the new machine age.

There is no sharp break between the work that Léger produced in the 1920s and what he did in the 1930s, but there are interesting modifications. For example, Léger painted a long series of still lifes with floating objects. The shallow space and tilted planes mark Léger out as being, like Braque, one of those who continued the explorations of Cubism. But certain features acknowledge the influence of the Surrealists – notably the striking disproportions of scale, the deliberate incongruity of certain images (the Mona Lisa with a huge bunch of keys), and the presence of abstract, biomorphic shapes. These still lifes alternate with pictures showing heavy, brutally outlined classical figures, which certainly owe something to the 'neo-classical' Picasso of

93

164

the early 1920s. The unifying factor is Léger's own graphism – his use of lines as heavy and black as those employed by Mondrian.

The Social Realist tendency did not appear in Léger's work until the late 1940s, and only affirmed itself fully with *Les Constructeurs* in 1950. This is all the more curious because he was involved with various political initiatives throughout the 1930s. In particular, Léger was a close friend of the Communist deputy and poet Paul Vaillant-Couturier who in 1932 (with Louis Aragon as one of his collaborators) helped to found the Association d'Écrivains et d'Artistes Révolution-naires. Léger was a member of this from the beginning, and it is clear that he felt strongly about the principles the association professed. In 1937 he said, in the course of a lecture given in Antwerp: 'Painters must place themselves at the disposition of organisers of popular festivals . . . to co-ordinate the overall planning of colour, for example, if that is what is required.' He was as good as his word. In the same year he planned the décor for the Congress of the C.G.T (the French Council of Trade Unions), held in Paris in the Vélodrome d'Hiver. He thus followed in the footsteps of his illustrious predecessor J. L. David, who planned and designed festivals for the French Revolution.

Yet, despite the increasing tensions of the political situation, activities of this kind remained very much on the margins of Léger's life during the decade. Apart from the work he did in the studio – undoubtedly most important of all to him – his main preoccupations were his activity as a teacher and his exhibitions and commissions in the United States, where he spent a great deal of time, and where he had many friends. The Museum of Modern Art in New York gave him a retrospective in 1935, and this was followed by one at the Chicago Art Institute. In 1938 he returned to America to decorate the apartment of Nelson Rockefeller. His success in the United States, and the fact that he received Rockefeller patronage, prompts a comparison with Diego Rivera, whom he in some ways resembles in style – but it is clear that Léger was, from the point of view of his American hosts, a much less controversial figure.

England: The Struggle to be Modern

The 1920s had been a torpid period in English art. The conservatism that affected the visual arts throughout Europe after World War I was especially strongly felt in England. The avant-garde impulse that had briefly surfaced just as the war began – an impulse typified by Vorticism – did not survive the conflict. During the decade that followed the war, enlightened English opinion on the visual arts was largely formed by members of the Bloomsbury group. Two of the circle, Roger Fry and Clive Bell, were influential critics; other Bloomsbury writers also concerned themselves from time to time with painting and sculpture. Fry occupied a key position because he had been largely responsible for introducing French Post-Impressionism to the British public. Like Bell, he thought of French art as being inherently superior to its British equivalent.

Fry was himself a practising painter, though a very dull one. The group also contained a number of other artists, and naturally these attracted the attention and sympathy of their writer friends, though always with the unspoken reservation that they were English rather than French, and thus necessarily of comparatively minor importance. The most prolific as well as the most prominent of the Bloomsbury artists were Vanessa Bell and Duncan Grant. Vanessa Bell was Virginia Woolf's sister. She was married to Clive Bell, though by 1930 they no longer lived together as man and wife. She had at one time been Roger Fry's mistress, but Grant was now her companion, and her daughter Angelica was in fact his child, though this was not publicly acknowledged. To add to the complications, Grant was by temperament homosexual, and had enjoyed relationships with many of the male members of the Bloomsbury circle, among them the great economist Maynard Keynes.

Their private lives were a good deal more adventurous than the art they produced. After a brief experimental period, both Bell and Grant had lapsed into a tempered, not to say tepid, version of the kind of Continental painting that Fry had taught them both to admire. It was a style that appealed to the cultivated public, and at the beginning of the 1930s both painters were at the height of their reputations – frequently exhibited and much praised when they were. Despite the

102

103

101. Wyndham Lewis
Stephen Spender, 1938

Oil on canvas
39½ × 23½in/105 × 169cm
City Museum and Art Galleries,
Stoke-on-Trent

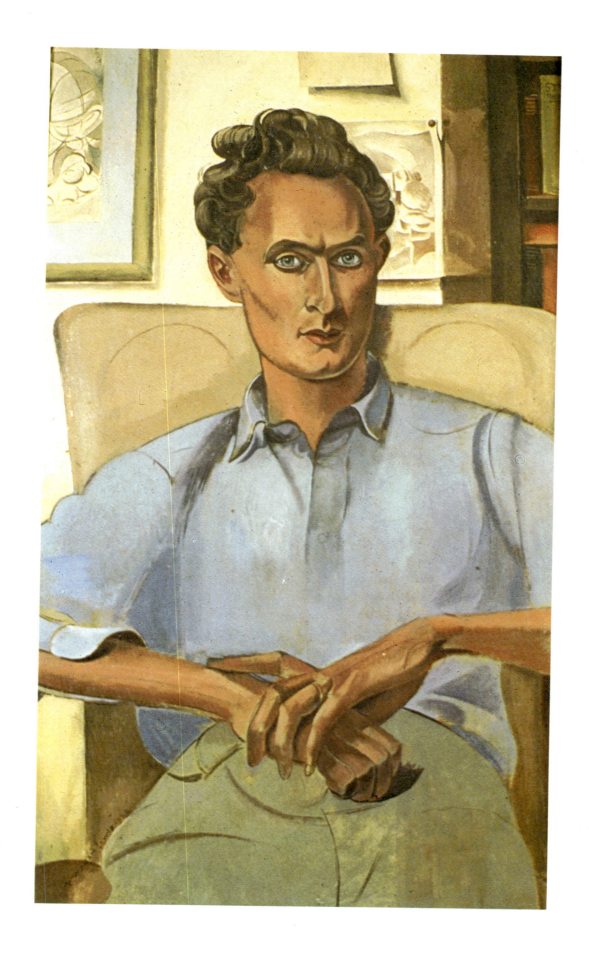

102. Roger Fry
Bridge over the Allier, c. 1933

Oil on canvas
12$\frac{3}{8}$ × 16$\frac{1}{8}$in/31.4 × 41cm
The Tate Gallery, London

worsening economic climate, their work sold reasonably well. Buyers found comfort and reassurance in what they produced – quiet still lifes, and glimpses of their own domestic surroundings. They also had a reputation as decorative artists, built up since the days of the Omega Workshops founded by Fry. In the mid-1930s, they were both commissioned to provide decorations for the new and much-publicized liner *Queen Mary*. But here their success received a check as what they produced was not liked, and Grant's large panels were totally rejected.

In public, their one outspoken opponent was Wyndham Lewis, the founder of Vorticism, who in 1930 published his savagely satirical novel *The Apes of God*, which lampooned Vanessa and Clive Bell in addition to many others. Wyndham Lewis, too, continued to paint, but grew less and less prolific as well as becoming more conservative in style. Nevertheless his fine portrait of Stephen Spender, done in 1938, shows that he was still capable of producing outstanding work. The problem was that he now shared the isolation that had overtaken so many leading artists in the Britain of the time.

Isolation did not always go hand in hand with lack of notice. One of the leading artists working in Britain during the inter-war period was Jacob Epstein. Epstein was in no danger of being ignored, but the atmosphere surrounding him was one that was positively unhelpful to

101

168

103. Duncan Grant
*The Harbour Master's Office,
Falmouth*, 1934

Oil on canvas
$14\frac{1}{4} \times 16$in/36.8×40.6cm
Christie's

a true appreciation of his art. His original reputation had been made as a carver in stone, hewing images from the block. He now reverted, at least for a large part of his production, to sculpture in bronze, very much in the tradition of Rodin, against whom he had once rebelled. He built up a large and immensely successful practice as a portrait sculptor – a Joshua Reynolds working in three dimensions. In 1939 *Picture Post* remarked that Epstein had been 'commissioned to do in bronze the heads of more celebrities than any sculptor in Britain. Conrad, Einstein, the Emperor of Abyssinia, Ramsay MacDonald, J. B. Priestley are only a few of them.'

Despite this he remained a violently controversial artist, and there were successive 'scandals' throughout the inter-war period stirred up by his large religious and allegorical pieces: the carvings of *Day* and *Night* on the Underground Headquarters Building near St James's Park, unveiled in 1929; followed by *Genesis* (1930–31), *Ecce Homo* (1934–5), *Consummatum Est* (1936–7), and *Adam* (1938–9). As Epstein bitterly recalls in his *Autobiography*, each of these in turn was greeted with volleys of abuse. A good deal of this came from people who ought to have known better. For the *Catholic Times*, *Ecce Homo* had 'the

104

105

169

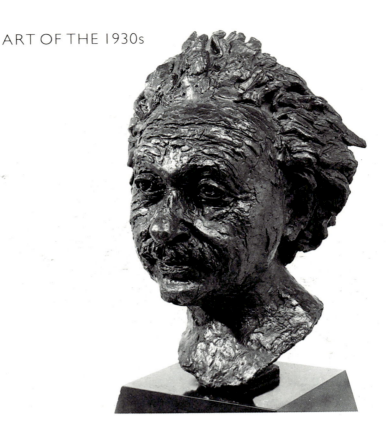

104. Jacob Epstein
Albert Einstein, 1933

Bronze
17in/43.1cm high
Christie's

debased, sensuous, flat features of an Asiatic monstrosity'. G. K. Chesterton said of the same figure:

> It is an outrage, and I admired *The Daily Mirror* for refusing to publish a picture of the statue. It is the greatest insult to religion I have ever seen, and will offend the religious feelings of the whole community.

Genesis had fared even worse in 1931. The *Daily Express* headed its review 'EPSTEIN'S BAD JOKE IN STONE', and sub-headed it 'Mongolian Moron that is Obscene'. The *Daily Telegraph* called it 'A Statue Unfit to Show' and the *Daily Mail* said 'it is difficult to imagine what defence can be offered for this simian-like creature whose face suggests, if anything, the missing link.'

There are distinct resemblances here to the kind of thing Nazi racial theoreticians said about the art of the Weimar Republic, and Epstein, as a Jew, must have felt doubly threatened as a result. The important point of resemblance, however, between Epstein's art and things condemned by the Nazis in Germany is not the sculptor's Jewishness, but his innate Expressionism. Epstein's religious sculptures and allegories are highly charged, and they arouse equally charged reactions from their audience. They are also works with strong links to the nineteenth century: the content is both specific and important. Clearly those who detested them were as much outraged by the content as they were by Epstein's style. English art-criticism, ever

105. Jacob Epstein
Consummatum Est, 1936–7

Alabaster
87$\frac{15}{16}$in/223.5cm long
Edinburgh National Galleries of
Scotland

since the days of Ruskin, has always had an innate moralism, and easily definable content offers an excuse for this. A work of art which the critic dislikes is frequently characterized as something actually wicked, rather than as something trivial, vulgar or foolish. Epstein thus often found himself pilloried in an especially personal and wounding way. But there was always something that communicated itself to an audience, however prejudiced – the works I have cited invariably drew large crowds when they were first exhibited. These attendances also owed something to the incoherent anger of many of his reviewers, which in this respect proved counter-productive.

What value do Epstein's major pieces have, now that all the fuss has died down? It is possible to argue that the sculptor's ambitions were greater than his capacity and that by and large he over-reached himself. Hugh Gordon Porteous, dismissed by Epstein as a lukewarm highbrow, clearly had something like this in mind when he reviewed the first showing of *Consummatum Est* for *The New English Weekly*:

One of the disadvantages of attempting anything on the gigantic scale is that, if it doesn't quite 'come off', there is a natural temptation to pass it off, even upon oneself, as if it had. It must be extremely galling for a man who has spent months or years of hard labour in hacking a cliff into the semblance of a figure, or in painting an acre of canvas, or in writing a million-word book, to find at the

171

106. Walter Richard Sickert
High Steppers, 1938–9

Oil on canvas
52 × 48¾in/132 × 124cm
Edinburgh National Galleries of
Scotland

end of it all the thing has failed. Even to recognize that fact for oneself would take a good deal more honesty and courage than common men possess. And it is only the rare artist who has the nerve to destroy in such cases. On the analogy of 'prevention is better than cure', the colossal in art should perhaps be avoided always. The urge 'to do something big' is a constant spur to genius. It is, however, a pity that it should so often take the unfortunate form of something merely *physically* big.

Today Epstein's huge carvings look the more impressive each time one encounters them. They have glaring faults, but these are compensated for by the generosity of Epstein's ambition, his vision of what art can achieve. One reason why they are so little discussed in relation to the rest of the art produced in Britain during the 1930s is that they tend to dwarf most of it spiritually as well as physically.

Another major, but isolated, artist working in Britain at this time was Stanley Spencer. Few painters have proved more resistant to categorization, and this, coupled with Spencer's own notorious eccentricity, has led to his being dismissed as a no doubt striking, but somehow 'unintelligent' artist, whose work can be regarded as marginal. The sheer quality of the images he produced makes this proposition untenable.

Where Epstein was an immigrant, British only by adoption, Spencer was native English. All his life he remained deeply rooted in the Thameside village of Cookham where he had been born. His imagination clung to it, even when he was forced to reside elsewhere. Despite his eventual isolation, his formation as an artist was very similar to that of a number of his contemporaries. He trained, immediately before World War I, at the Slade School, University College of London, where he received a thorough grounding in academic draughtsmanship, and his early work was heavily influenced by Pre-Raphaelitism which still, in the early part of the century, retained an extraordinary grip on English art. In Spencer's case the influence of the Pre-Raphaelites was reinforced by his own natural mysticism.

During the 1930s Spencer's private life passed through a violent crisis. He had finished his paintings for the Burghclere Memorial Chapel, which embodied his vision of World War I. He then returned to Cookham, and became infatuated with Patricia Preece, whom he married in 1937, after divorcing his first wife Hilda. He would have preferred to maintain a relationship with both women simultaneously. The second marriage was soon revealed as a mockery and Spencer found himself exiled to Hampstead, where he continued to see and correspond with Hilda, who was living in the same district of London with her family. All of these events were incorporated into his art.

Spencer's paintings of the 1930s cover a wide stylistic range. There are the realistic landscapes he painted for money – these seem to have a kinship with the German 'Magic Realism' of the 1920s. There are erotic nudes of Patricia Preece, the best-known of which is the so-called *Leg of Mutton Nude* (1937), which incorporates Spencer's own

173

6

self-portrait. There are pictures that in different ways express the artist's notion of universal love. An example is *The Dustman, or the Lovers*, (1935) which Spencer described as '... the glorifying and magnifying of a dustman. The joy of his bliss is spiritual in his union with his wife who carries him in her arms and experiences the bliss of union with his corduroy trousers ...' Of the figures proffering items salvaged from the dustbins he said: 'Nothing I love is rubbish and so I resurrect the teapot and the empty jam tin, and the cabbage stalks, and as there is a mystery in the Trinity, so there is in these three and many others of no apparent significance.' The figure holding the teapot aloft is in fact another self-portrait.

The Dustman, or the Lovers, unlike the landscapes and nudes, shows a strong degree of expressive distortion, and this was certainly one of the reasons – quite apart from its curious subject-matter – why it was rejected (to Spencer's fury) by the Royal Academy Hanging Committee of 1935. Today this seems a strange decision. The picture is consistent within itself, and has a strong, coherent and original plastic language, quite unlike anything being produced at the same time in either Europe or the United States.

Another important painter who pursued a solitary course during the 1930s was Walter Richard Sickert. Sickert had been the founder of the Camden Town Group and was a direct link between English artists and Degas. Around 1927 his art suddenly entered a new phase – one till recently dismissed by most critics as a sad decline. He became more and more dependent on ready-made images – photographs, press-clippings and banal nineteenth-century engravings – and his touch became increasingly 'raw'. These apparent faults are now construed by some of his admirers as virtues in their own right. In his foreword to the *Late Sickert*, an exhibition presented by the Arts Council of Great Britain in 1981, the painter Frank Auerbach wrote:

> If one were to ascribe a development to him, one might say that Sickert became less interested in composition, that is in selection, arrangement and presentation, devoted himself, more and more, to a direct transformation of whatever came accidentally to hand and

107. William Roberts
Playground, 1936

Oil on canvas
$56\frac{3}{8} \times 62\frac{3}{4}$in/$143 \times 159$cm
The Tate Gallery, London

engaged his interest, and accepted the haphazard variety of his unprocessed subject-matter.

In doing this, Sickert (so it is said) anticipated some of the preoccupations of leading artists in the 1980s.

The results of Sickert's stylistic transformation seem to me to be mixed. A large number of the 'Echoes' taken from Victorian sources fail to transcend the banality of their originals, and exude, in addition, an embarrassing facetiousness. But any important artist deserves to be judged by his best rather than his worst work, and at the end of his life Sickert undoubtedly produced a handful of fine, and totally original pictures. At a time when it was in steep decline, he managed to revive the venerable tradition of the large, full-length portrait. His likenesses of Lord Castlerosse (1935), Lord Farington (c. 1936), and above all of Edward VIII (1936) – taken either from snapshots or press photographs – preserve the immediacy of the photographic image and give it a hallucinatory vividness, an effect intensified by the strange, harsh, bright and bleak colour schemes he used, and by his peremptory handling, which catches some of the spirit of late Titian.

Another fine picture is *High Steppers* of 1938–9, which depicts a row **106** of chorus girls. This, once again based on a photograph, abandons the

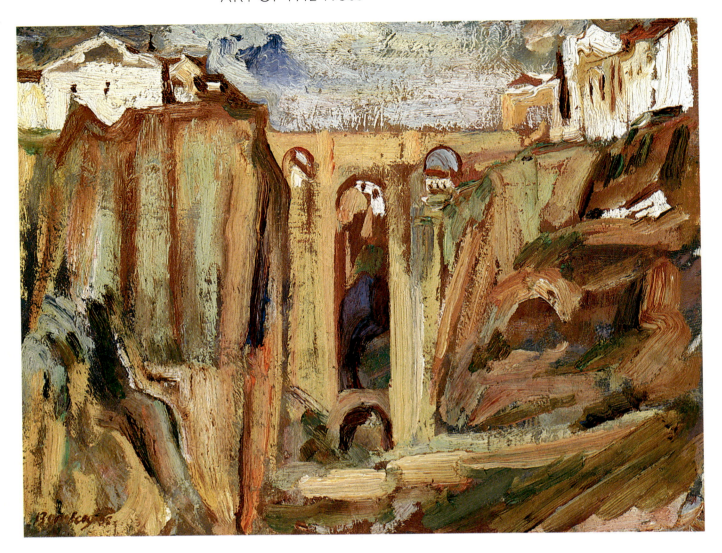

108. David Bomberg
Ronda Bridge, 1935

Oil on panel
12 × 16in/31 × 41cm
Courtesy of Fischer Fine Art Ltd

107

immediacy of the music-hall scenes Sickert had painted much earlier in his career in favour of a successful attempt to produce an evenly animated surface that can be read almost in the same terms as one reads an abstract picture. There is here a strange anticipation of the 'Flags' painted by the American Neo-Dadaist Jasper Johns at the end of the 1950s.

Also isolated stylistically from the rest of the British art-world were two ex-Vorticists. The less important was William Roberts, who had by this time developed a consistent but monotonous stylization of the human figure which owed more than a little to Léger in its use of tubular forms. Roberts used this convention as the basis of crowded multi-figure compositions which, for all their superficial air of modernity, hark back to Victorian narrative painting. The ingenuity of his designs is vitiated by an almost total lack of inflection in the actual handling of the paint. A comparison with Stanley Spencer, who also seems to echo Léger at certain moments, demonstrates Spencer's great superiority.

David Bomberg, who had painted some of the most ambitious Vorticist compositions, among them *The Mud Bath* (1914) now in the Tate, pursued a very different course from Roberts. He abandoned the mechanistic, semi-abstract style he had once practised in favour of broad painterliness. He rejected both Cubism and Expressionism as these are conventionally understood in favour of his own interpretation of the legacy of Cézanne. 'We conceive of art,' Bomberg said once, 'as the incomprehensible density of cosmic forces compressed into a small space.' During the 1930s Bomberg spent much of his time abroad – he was often in Spain, and he also travelled to Morocco, the Greek Islands and Russia. Though he had three exhibitions in London during the decade (1932, 1936 and 1937), his art was little appreciated and he was often in severe financial straits. His bombastic and aggressive personality undoubtedly created difficulties for him that a man of different temperament might have avoided. It was only after World War II, when Bomberg taught for a spell at the Borough Polytechnic in London, that he collected a group of young disciples around himself. Thanks to their efforts, the importance of his post-Vorticist work began at long last to be appreciated. Much post-war British figurative painting is directly dependent on it. The combination of Cézanne's ideas with a nature-mysticism which comes from Blake now seems typical of the decade when some of Bomberg's best work – for example his powerful landscapes of Ronda – was being done in almost total obscurity. The artist wrote, in an undated note discovered after his death in 1957:

108

In Art are other manifestations of the Gravitational forces at work – The revolutions birth and Death ways and means of making and seeing and forming I conceive as having their Origin and being Subject to forces that regulate the seasons the winds Tides and Ocean swell – we may be Realists Mystics or Romantics or all three – But it is with these reasons when we are impelled to Draw or Paint

109. Matthew Smith
Reclining Nude, 1931–2

Oil on canvas
$21\frac{1}{2} \times 25\frac{1}{4}$in/54.6 × 64.1cm
Christie's

or Sculpt that we approach the mass to write in harmony Spirit and Matter – Can mechanisation deprive of these Human things are we to lose our Eden –

109 At first sight, Matthew Smith's heavily worked, painterly style seems to mark him out as the direct rival of Bomberg, and there are other similarities as well – chief among them the fact that Smith spent much time out of England during the 1930s – in fact, even more than Bomberg did. He was resident in France throughout the decade, working first in Paris, then at Cannes, then from 1934–40 at Aix-en-Provence. But where Bomberg travelled to escape the shadow of the great French masters of the nineteenth and twentieth centuries, Matthew Smith wanted to identify with them. Bomberg frequently strove towards something he lacked the means to achieve – an idea that existed in his own mind; Smith on the other hand strove towards a kind of painting already fully realized by Matisse and Bonnard.

110 A similar fault, but in even more obvious form, mars the work of Glyn Philpot, who at the beginning of the 1930s abandoned a career as a fashionable academic portrait painter in order to attempt something more radical. It was a courageous decision, not altogether rewarded by the results. The best of the figure compositions Philpot produced in

110. Glyn Philpot
Acrobats Waiting to Rehearse,
1935

Oil on canvas
$45\frac{5}{8} \times 35\frac{3}{16}$in/116 × 89.4cm
Borough of Brighton Royal
Pavilion Art Gallery & Museums

the last phase of his career are as heavily dependent on the Picasso of the Blue and Rose periods as Matthew Smith was on Matisse. Between them the two artists justify Clive Bell's gloomy certainty that British painters would always be inherently inferior to their French equivalents. Philpot's work is nevertheless worth a historical footnote, as it demonstrates how the style favoured by Balthus, Tchelitchew and Bérard in France found a foothold on the other side of the Channel.

At first sight completely out of the Modernist mainstream, but nevertheless perfectly convincing in its own terms, is the work of an

179

artist who caused much less stir than Philpot in the inter-war period, even though he showed regularly at the Royal Academy Summer exhibition. This is Meredith Frampton, who is only now beginning to be rediscovered. Frampton was a meticulous craftsman, whose work proceeded so slowly that he never, during the whole of his active career (which came to a conclusion in 1945), accumulated enough work for a one-person exhibition. His portraits and rare still lifes and subject pictures have a crystalline precision that now impresses many viewers. Their lack of modernity is more apparent than actual – they are in fact closely related to the return to realism experienced throughout Europe during the 1920s and 1930s. Frampton's later paintings are particularly close to those of the German Christian Schad and the Dutchman Carel Willink. What they all have in common is a precision that pushes 'realistic' representation beyond its own boundaries, and endows it with a transcendental quality. Frampton achieves this not only through unerring precision of drawing, but through his control of colour and tone. These are the most genuinely luminous paintings produced in England throughout the decade.

111

The huge gulf in style that exists between the Expressionist carvings of Epstein on the one hand and the classical realism of Frampton on the other indicates the wide range of options open to English artists during the decade. At the same time it signals the difficulty these artists had in creating a visual language that would strike spectators as something completely appropriate to their time and situation. The hostility aspiring Modernists experienced was the reaction of a public even more uncertain than they were themselves about what the future contained, and apt to respond with disproportionate rage to art that symbolized the changes being wrought in society by forces outside their control. The attempts made by various British painters and sculptors to confront this situation is the subject of my next chapter.

111. Meredith Frampton
Portrait of a Young Woman,
1935

Oil on canvas
81 × 42½in/205 × 108cm
The Tate Gallery, London

English Abstract Art

The Seven & Five Society, founded in 1919, was, together with the short-lived X Group, founded at the same period, the first attempt made in England to revive the spirit of avant-gardism after the hiatus imposed by the war. The Seven & Five continued, in large part because it was careful not to aim very high. The manifesto printed in the catalogue of its first exhibition, held in April 1920, is quite frank about this lack of ambition:

> The 'SEVEN & FIVE' are grateful to the pioneers, but feel that there has been of late too much pioneering along too many lines in altogether too much of a hurry, and themselves desire the pursuit of their own calling rather than the confusion of conflict.

The only significant name among the early members is that of Ivon Hitchens. Through Hitchens, Ben Nicholson, then just beginning his career as a painter, was asked to become a member, and he exhibited with the Society for the first time at its fifth exhibition, held in 1924.

Gradually new wine was poured into the old bottle. Nicholson was joined by other pioneering Modernists: his first wife, Winifred Nicholson; his second wife, Barbara Hepworth; Frances Hodgkins, Henry Moore and John Piper. The great majority of these did not arrive until the early 1930s, which accurately reflected the gradual change of climate that was taking place in the English art-world.

The Seven & Five held its last exhibition in 1935, but by that time it had already been challenged by the much more radical Unit One. Unit One provided a much better guide to the new avant-garde, then in the process of formation, after the long doldrum of the 1920s. The membership consisted of two architects – Welles Coates and Colin Lucas; seven painters – Edward Wadsworth, Ben Nicholson, Paul Nash, Tristram Hillier, Edward Burra, John Bigge and John Armstrong; and two sculptors – Henry Moore and Barbara Hepworth. The list thus included the majority of those who were to help give a new and more coherent orientation to British art.

Some of the leading figures in Unit One were already mature and established artists at the time of its foundation. One such was Edward Wadsworth, already in his mid-forties. Wadsworth studied at the

112. Edward Wadsworth
Dux et Comes, 1933

Tempera
$14\frac{3}{4} \times 20\frac{1}{2}$in/37.5 × 52cm
Courtesy of Marlborough Fine Art
(London) Ltd

Slade at the same time as Stanley Spencer; showed at the Second Post-Impressionist Exhibition of 1913, organized by Roger Fry; worked briefly with the Omega Workshops, and was one of the founder-members of the Vorticist group. During the 1920s he travelled frequently to Paris. Giorgio de Chirico, Léger, the sculptor Ossip Zadkine and the dealers Léonce and Paul Rosenberg were among his friends there.

During the late 1920s Wadsworth painted a series of marine still lifes which were strongly influenced by de Chirico. Now, in the early 1930s, he was veering towards abstraction, attracted by Ozenfant and Léger. Answering a series of questions put to him by the magazine *The Studio* in October 1933, Wadsworth said: 'I maintain that Art is the continuation of Nature, which that artist uses as an instrument to help him create parallel with nature . . . At no period has the aspect of things been a main consideration in my painting, though admittedly I have from time to time been stimulated by certain landscapes or objects, the realistic appearance of which I have promptly subdued in order to emphasize qualities I consider more important.'

In effect Wadsworth's so-called 'abstractions' are seldom completely abstract. The exceptions are a small group of paintings which use biomorphic forms derived not from Ozenfant and from Léger but from the wooden reliefs of Arp. Most of his paintings at this period consist of patterns created from simplifications of pre-existing forms. One *Composition* (1930) takes as its *donnée* a multi-bladed penknife, blades partly extended and repeated several times, on each occasion on a different scale. This form is paired with simplified representations of geometrical instruments.

Wadsworth was not able to push his experiments further, and in 1934 he abruptly abandoned the attempt, and returned to the marine themes he had used previously. These now made him an ally of the Surrealists. His connection with them is emphasized by the work of his close friend Tristram Hillier, who at this time described some of his paintings as 'Surrealist landscapes'. They are no more and no less so than Wadsworth's marines, which Hillier sometimes imitated very ably. His impressive painting *Le Havre de Grâce* of 1939 is scarcely distinguishable from Wadsworth's own work, so skilfully does it use his characteristic themes.

Wadsworth's eclecticism – his tendency to veer from style to style – gives one the impression that he knew very well what Modernism was about, but had not the conviction to commit himself fully to any one aspect of it. His work consistently falls short of what one feels he might have achieved.

This is not true of Paul Nash, who had been another contemporary of Spencer and Wadsworth at the Slade. Nash took what had originally seemed a modest talent and stretched it to its limits. As his early drawings show, he had been particularly enamoured of the Pre-Raphaelites as a young man, and some of their romanticism still clings to his work throughout its subsequent development. In the early 1930s Nash, like Wadsworth, possessed a well-established name. In 1931 he was invited to America to serve on the jury of the Carnegie

113. Paul Nash
Landscape from a Dream,
1936–8

Oil on canvas
$26\frac{3}{4} \times 40$in/68×101cm
The Tate Gallery, London

International Award. In 1932 he was elected President and Chairman of the Council of the Society of Industrial Artists. In the same year he worked as art-critic of *The Listener*, where he alternated with Herbert Read; and in 1933 it was he who announced the foundation of Unit One in a letter to *The Times*.

During this period, however, Nash was in poor health, and this fact, coupled with all his other activities, tended to restrict his output. His health did not improve – he suffered from bronchial asthma – but he managed to be more productive after 1934. In April of that year he wrote to Anthony Bertram, who was later to be his biographer:

I feel I am beginning now to find my way between the claims of 'Abstraction' and pure interpretation. As you know, I am far too interested in the character of landscape and natural forms generally – from a pictorial point of view – ever to abandon painting *after* Nature of some kind or another. But I want a wider aspect, a different angle of vision as it were. This I am beginning to find through symbolism and in the power of association – not the rather

114. Paul Nash
Equivalents for the Megaliths,
1935

Oil on canvas
18 × 26in/45.7 × 66cm
The Tate Gallery, London

freakish unlikely association of objects, so much as the *right* association as I feel it to be . . . I desire to penetrate further – or if you like to fling my net wider to include a relationship of spiritual personality – only I suppose I must find another word for spiritual, or be misunderstood.

Early on in the 1930s Nash had begun to be interested in Surrealism. In 1933 he wrote an article in which he wholeheartedly praised the work of Max Ernst, and in 1936 he was a member of the committee of the International Surrealist Exhibition held in London, which caused an immense stir. But he never committed himself completely to the Surrealist programme – its influence meant for him 'the release of imprisoned thoughts of poetry and fantasy', and in this respect the English Romantics of the early nineteenth century remained a more important example than anything borrowed from abroad. Particularly characteristic of this period in Nash's work are landscapes organized and animated by some Object (Nash himself insisted on the capital letter and was delighted when the Belgian Surrealist René Magritte nicknamed him 'The Master of the Object'). These Objects provided Nash with a way of marrying Surrealist practice to a more traditional kind of English nature mysticism. Many compositions of this type were inspired by the landscape round Swanage in Dorset where Nash, always peripatetic though now confined to England by his ill-health, based himself for a year or two during the mid-1930s.

113

114

186

Nash's work as a landscapist marks the beginnings of a romantic revival in English art that did not reach its height until the war years, when England was isolated from the Continent. Two other artists closely associated with this movement were John Piper and Graham Sutherland. Piper, who began as a provincial imitator of Picasso and Léger, was eventually to develop into the most skilful topographical watercolourist of his generation, giving new life to a traditional English genre. Sutherland is a more complex case. He had begun his career as an artist in the late 1920s, profiting from the short-lived boom in modern prints that preceded the Slump. He was then little more than a skilful imitator of Samuel Palmer. The sudden collapse of the print market forced him to remake his career as an artist and this he did with some success, producing a series of visionary oil and watercolour landscapes of Pembrokeshire in which Palmer's influence, though still very much present, is more successfully concealed. Sutherland at this period had the good luck to attract two rich and influential patrons – Kenneth Clark and Colin Anderson, who were among the few men in their position in England to take a close interest

115. Graham Sutherland
Pembrokeshire Landscape,
1936

Pen, ink and gouache
$14 \times 21\frac{1}{2}$in/35.5×54.6cm
Cardiff National Museum, Wales
(Visual Arts Library)

115

187

in modern art. The work he produced in response to their interest was probably the best of his whole career. But even the most successful of his Welsh landscapes fail to conceal a certain fumbling tentativeness that was to become more painfully conspicuous when Sutherland later attempted to work on a more ambitious scale. The quarrel over his ultimate status is still unsettled, and is of course complicated by work produced a long time after the period under review, notably the series of portraits of celebrities which for a while made Sutherland one of the best-known of English contemporary painters.

The greatest name among the experimental artists of the period is undoubtedly that of Henry Moore, who can also be connected with renewed upsurge of romantic feeling in English art. The year 1931 marked a break in Moore's development. During the second half of the 1920s he had already reached the first phase of his maturity as an artist, producing carved figures and heads that put him in the first rank of modern sculptors. The influences he had already absorbed were very diverse. They ranged from those of slightly senior contemporaries such as Constantin Brancusi and Alexander Archipenko to sculpture from various primitive civilizations. A reclining Maya Chac-Mool particularly obsessed Moore at this epoch and provided the inspiration for his earliest reclining figures.

117 Now, in the 1930s, Moore was still working chiefly as a carver, but the work he produced showed a much more plastic and organic interpretation of nature. The new forms he uses are biomorphic metaphors for nature rather than direct representations of nature itself. The reclining figures and other characteristic motifs remain, but are now treated in a much freer way. A reclining figure, for example, may now consist of three of four separate masses, united only by a common base. Moore's work at this period is endlessly inventive formally – the sculptures are sometimes closed and block-like, sometimes rhythmical and flowing, with shapes suggested by the materials from which they are made. They refer to a wide variety of natural phenomena: to the human form, to animals, and often to landscape, which Moore equates with the human, and especially the female figure.

116. John Piper
*Hartwell Church,
Buckinghamshire,* 1939

Oil on board
$22 \times 16\frac{1}{4}$in/56×40.7cm
Lincoln, Usher Gallery

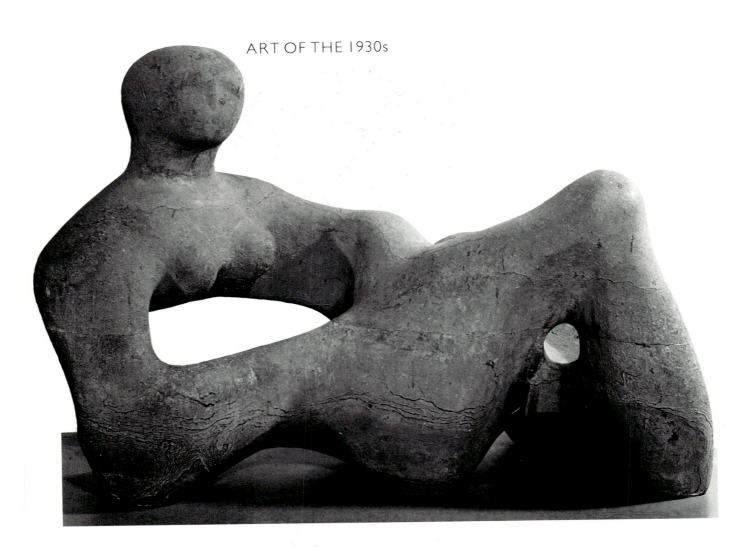

117. Henry Moore
Recumbent Figure, 1938

Stone
$35 \times 52\frac{1}{4} \times 29$in/$89 \times 132.7 \times 73.6$cm
The Tate Gallery, London

118. Henry Moore
The Bride, 1939–40

Lead and wire
92in/233.6cm high
The Museum of Modern Art, New
York/Henry Moore Foundation

In the mid-1930s, after he had acquired a cottage at Kingston, near Canterbury, with a large field attached to it, Moore was able to fulfil a long-cherished ambition. This was to produce sculptures large enough to make their point in the open air, in relation to landscape. In this sense they are like scaled-up versions of the Objects which Paul Nash imagined for his paintings. They are also much more than this comparison suggests – an attempt at a deliberately monumental art whose ambitions surpassed even those of Epstein.

It is in his attitudes towards landscape that Moore prompts a comparison with Nash and even with Sutherland. But he is always, within the period, a more radical artist than either of them, and other aspects of his work demonstrate both the breadth of his thinking and the wide variety of his interests. In the late 1930s he produced a series of stringed figures which are now among his best-known images. They were originally suggested by mathematical models seen in the Science Museum, London. There are several possible explanations for Moore's use of stringing – there is the suggestion, for instance, that the

sculpture is a musical instrument, something not only harmonious to look at but capable of producing harmonies when touched. But the strings also have a different function: they veil the form they surround (one of Moore's stringed pieces, 1939–40, is actually called *The Bride*), and they separate one space from another, the space contained within the sculpture from the space outside. The 1930s were the period when Moore developed the preoccupation with the relationships between inner and outer that has continued to characterize his work.

The strings themselves were not a device Moore himself employed for long. One reason for giving them up may have been the fact that Barbara Hepworth, who began to employ them about the same time, continued to use them. Moore remarked later, and there is something contemptuous in his tone: 'When the war came I gave up this type of thing. Others, like Gabo and Hepworth, have gone on using it. It becomes a matter of ingenuity rather than of fundamental human experience.'

If Moore felt at least the occasional prick of jealousy where Hepworth was concerned, it would not be surprising. Next to himself, she was the most distinguished English sculptor of the period. Hepworth's earliest independent work, produced in the late 1920s, was influenced by both Epstein and Moore. But it was nevertheless she, rather than Moore, who was responsible for inventing a device later to be associated in the public mind with both of them – the hole pierced through the form. Hepworth made her first carving of this sort in 1931.

In 1932 she joined her fortunes, personal and artistic, with those of Ben Nicholson, and this made a marked difference to the direction she took. Though never becoming servile imitators of Continental fashions, she and Nicholson were in constant dialogue with what was happening in Europe, consciously rejecting some parts of it, accepting and refining others. It is no accident that Hepworth's carvings, from 1933 onwards, become considerably more abstract. In some, she makes use of regular geometric forms – the cylinder, the sphere and the half-sphere – things that never appear in Moore's work. In addition, her imagery is much less tied to the human body. What

continues to link her to Moore is her feeling for landscape. Some of her most striking carvings, such as the *Discs in Echelon* of 1935, can be interpreted in terms of Palmeresque nature-mysticism – as an allusion to an eclipse of the moon. Her work was never to be so sensitive again.

Hepworth's husband (her second, just as she was his second wife), Ben Nicholson, was the most combative member of the English avant-garde at this period and one of the most energetic organizers of artists' groups. Unlike Moore, or Hepworth herself, he had been brought up in an artistic milieu. His father was the well-known painter William Nicholson, remembered for his exquisite traditional still lifes, and his mother was the sister of another artist, James Pryde.

During the 1920s, Ben Nicholson evolved a style that combined traditional elements with others borrowed from Cézanne and the Cubists, and a dash of sophisticated primitivism. His subjects were landscape and still life, and the aim was to produce a very direct art,

119. Barbara Hepworth
Discs in Echelon, 1935

Padouk wood
$12\frac{1}{4}$in/31.1cm high, attached to base
$19\frac{3}{8} \times 8\frac{7}{8}$in/49.2 × 22.5cm
Collection, The Museum of Modern Art, New York. Gift of
W. B. Bennet

without any rhetoric – painting without upholstery, so to speak. The primitive aspect of Nicholson's art was reinforced by his discovery, in 1928, of the work of a genuine primitive painter, the old Cornish fisherman Alfred Wallis, who lived and worked at St Ives.

Nicholson's meeting with Barbara Hepworth, and their subsequent association, marked a new epoch for him as well as for her. 'The working-together in the same studio in those days was vital to my understanding of *form*,' he was to write later. 'In fact, the interchange of ideas without any "lifting" on either side was vital to us both.' Almost equally vital was direct contact with the Paris art milieu. In 1932 the Nicholsons went to Paris and met Picasso, Braque, Brancusi and Arp. In 1933, they returned, and this time met Mondrian. They themselves created a favourable impression and they were invited to join Abstraction-Creation, the principal grouping of abstract artists in Paris at that time.

Nicholson, who had up to this point been purely a painter, and one who always retained figurative elements in his work, now started to make a series of white reliefs – the first of these was completed in December 1933. The point of reference for these was Mondrian, whom Nicholson rapidly came to know well. But, unlike Mondrian, he did not want his art to become impersonal – the reliefs retain a current of subdued romantic feeling that links them to the rest of the avant-garde work being produced in England at that time. Nicholson in any case did not give himself up to producing them at the expense of all other work. He continued to paint Cubistic still lifes, with a debt to Braque in particular, and he also began to make purely abstract paintings linked to the reliefs, with the same idea of creating what he called 'a poetic relationship' between forms.

Compared to their Continental counterparts, nearly all of Nicholson's paintings and reliefs of the 1930s possess a subtle irregularity – one might almost describe it as a kind of wilfulness – which signals their ultimate dependence on emotion rather than reason. There is also a characteristic modesty, a refusal to make large claims. Like the Bloomsbury Group painters, Nicholson retained an inhibiting awe of what had been achieved in France. His own

120

120. Ben Nicholson
White Relief, 1935

Oil on wood relief
$40 \times 65\frac{1}{2}$ in/101×166 cm
The Tate Gallery, London

achievement during the 1930s was striking, but he was only to discover fullest confidence in his own gifts when, at the outbreak of war, he and Hepworth were forced to take refuge at St Ives.

The work of Wadsworth, Nash, Moore, Hepworth or Ben Nicholson can be considered almost in isolation from the political events of the 1930s, and this is the way in which it has traditionally been treated. There was, however, a great deal of artistic activity during the decade that was politically inspired. The chief organ of political expression was the Artists International Association (AIA) founded in 1933. The artists who joined this covered a wide stylistic range. Nicholson himself was one of the members. But there was always a core of artists who worked in a Social Realist style. Among these was one of the founder members of the AIA, Clifford Rowe, who actually worked in Moscow for a brief period during 1932–3. His work is not experimental in any sense, but can achieve a striking monumentalism. Another artist who did good work in this manner was Percy Horton, and yet another was a Hungarian-Jewish refugee called Peter Peri, whose coloured concrete figures made polemical use of a material conventionally considered to be ignoble and unsuited to fine art.

The impact of the Social Realists within the AIA led to a renewed interest in realism in general. Hogarth became a popular subject for art-historical research, and there was a renewal of respect for Sickert, despite the eccentricity of some of his later production. The Marxist art-critics of the period, chief among them the young Anthony Blunt, even suggested that a reconciliation was now due between the Royal Academy and its opponents. In 1937, reviewing the RA Summer Exhibition of that year in *The Spectator*, Blunt wrote:

> The only hope for European painting at the present time is the development of a new realism. Abstract art is played out on the continent . . . The possibility of a useful development occurring from more or less conventional artists makes it again almost profitable to visit the Royal Academy.

What Blunt picked out on this occasion was the work of a number of young artists who belonged to the AIA and were exhibiting among the

121. Laura Knight
The Gypsy, c. 1939

Oil on canvas
24 × 16in/61 × 40.6cm
The Tate Gallery, London

196

Academicians. They included Roland Hilder, James Fitton, Carel Weight and Ruskin Spear. But even among the Academy's own membership there were artists who were prepared to link themselves to some of the AIA's political aims – one of these was the ever-popular Laura Knight.

121

Renewed interest in realism led eventually to the creation of an organization that aimed to teach sound realist principles in art. This was the Euston Road School, founded in 1937. The artists associated with it saw Sickert as their most immediate ancestor, and they received some support from the painters associated with Bloomsbury – Vanessa Bell and Duncan Grant are both named as sponsors in an early prospectus. The participants were William Coldstream, Graham Bell, Victor Pasmore, Geoffrey Tibble and Rodrigo Moynihan. Four of these – Bell, Tibble, Moynihan and Pasmore – had previously been involved in a rather different movement, which they labelled 'Objective Abstraction'. This was a somewhat timid attempt to create an abstract art that would be free and painterly, with no trace of the strict geometries of Mondrian. The artist who momentarily came closest to this aim was Moynihan, and the results were described by David Gascoyne (then only seventeen) in a review in the *New English Weekly*:

> He has achieved some very curious effects; as though a Kandinsky had been using the bleary technique of a Monet, with a range of pale dirty colours laid on very thickly . . .

Objective Abstraction proved to be a dead end, and it was a sign of a changing artistic climate when the participants reverted to figuration. There was a transitional period when some of them largely ceased to paint. In 1934–7 Graham Bell was chiefly preoccupied with journalism, and Coldstream, who had not actually participated in the abortive movement, though he knew the participants, worked for the GPO Film Unit under John Grierson. It was Coldstream who, during this period of inactivity, gradually elaborated a very different theoretical basis for the artist's activity, and in 1938 he painted a picture that makes a statement of the viewpoint he had succeeded in reaching – it shows the dreary backstreets of Bolton under a pall of smoke (National

Gallery of Canada, Ottawa). In his own mind the motivation for producing a work of this type, so resolutely un- or even anti-modern in surface appearance, was absolutely clear: 'The slump had made me aware of social problems, and I became convinced that art ought to be directed towards a wider public. Whereas all the ideas I had learned to be artistically revolutionary ran in the opposite direction. Public art must mean realism.'

The Euston Road School itself (named from its location, but also by analogy with the Camden Town Group) was a place where Coldstream did little direct teaching, but where he exercised a preponderant theoretical influence which was 'opposed to the aesthetics of discrimination and aesthetic of verification' – the phrase is that of Lawrence Gowing, an early pupil. Those connected with it aimed to produce a measured, exact, long-meditated figurative image. Startling

122. William Coldstream
Bolton, 1938

Oil on canvas
$28\frac{1}{4} \times 36$in/71.8×91.4cm
National Gallery of Canada, Ottawa; gift of the Massey Foundation, 1946

123. Edward Burra
Izzy Orts, c. 1937

Watercolour
29 × 41 in/74 × 104cm
Edinburgh National Gallery,
Scotland

subject-matter and bright colour were both avoided. There were, however, quite marked divisions of aim among the participants. Whereas Coldstream and Bell aimed at a more sophisticated version of Social Realism, linked to the native English tradition of Camden Town, Pasmore and one or two of the others remained in thrall to the man Sickert himself regarded as his master – that is, to Degas. The Euston Road School was short-lived – it closed soon after the outbreak of war. The paintings produced by the chief figures connected with it are isolated, for all their evident merits, within the European context. What gives the enterprise its importance is the influence it subsequently exercised over the teaching of art in England in the years after World War II. With the exception of Graham Bell, killed in 1943, almost all the leading figures connected with it went on to occupy influential positions in the art-teaching establishment.

It remains to say a word about one isolated and indeed eccentric figure, whose real importance as an artist has only come to be realized recently. This was Edward Burra, who associated with most of the leading avant-garde artists of his time, but whose style has little in common with theirs. Burra came from a prosperous family, and had no real financial problems, but suffered all his life from poor health. He found it exhausting to work in oils, and preferred the quintessentially English medium of watercolour, which he used to make large and elaborate compositions. His subject-matter during the 1930s seems at first sight to link him to artists of the German *Neue Sachlichkeit* — most of all to Georg Grosz — and he has sometimes been accused of being no more than a weaker version of these German forerunners. In fact, his aims were quite different — he was not a social critic but a purveyor of fantasies. The low-life scenes which formed his chief subject-matter in the early 1930s — brothels, nightclubs and sailors' cafés in Mediterranean port-towns, equivalent subjects in New York's Harlem and in Mexico — were interspersed with purely fantastic scenes, full of monsters and dancing skeletons. In fact, there is no real division between the two categories; both are embodiments of things imagined rather than representations rooted in reality. Burra successfully rebelled against the prevailing current of his time — his paintings, in their mixture of grim and gay, have a sly, beguiling childishness, a cunning blend of the sophisticated and the naïve which reminds me of the novels of Ronald Firbank. Both Aubrey Beardsley and Edward Burne-Jones can be numbered among Burra's artistic ancestors. The extraordinary thing is that, despite his fancifulness and his literariness, he is perhaps the English artist who best caught the spirit of the epoch.

123

Portugal, Latin America, Holland and Belgium in the 1930s

Art in the smaller countries of Europe, and in Latin America with the exception of Mexico, inevitably tended to follow patterns set in the great creative centres, and especially in France. Portugal is a good example, with a number of gifted painters following Paris fashions a little belatedly, but often managing to add something genuinely orginal of their own. The best-known Portuguese artist who came to **125** maturity at this period is Maria Helena Vieira da Silva. Vieira da Silva had the advantage of a long period of study and residence in Paris – she eventually became a French citizen. She worked first with the sculptors Charles Despiau and Émile-Antoine Bourdelle, and later with Émile-Othon Friesz and Fernand Léger. Her personal style was fully evolved by about 1936 and has not varied greatly since. Her typical works are abstract paintings full of strange vertiginous perspectives, where tiny patches of glowing colour are caught in a network of lines. There is usually a cryptic suggestion of a landscape motif. The painters who remained in Portugal were hardly touched by this very personal stylistic development. More typical and more central to the Portuguese situation is the work of Almada Negreiros, a generation older than Vieira da Silva and a favourite of the Salazar regime which ruled Portugal almost throughout the decade and for many years afterwards. Negreiros's work bears a distinct resemblance to the Italian Novecento, and this is not wholly surprising, since Salazar in many ways modelled himself on Mussolini, though he eschewed Mussolini's flamboyance. His imitation of Mussolini extended to his policy concerning the arts. In 1934, the year after the constitution of Salazar's *Estado Novo* was proclaimed, the dictator's henchman António Ferro was already busy declaring: 'As the Duce in Italy knew how to bring to light the ruins of Rome, so the new Portuguese state has brought about a remarkable achievement on behalf of the arts.' Ferro organized fourteen *Exposições de Arte Moderna* with official prizes at the Secretariado Nacional de Propaganda between 1935 and 1951. Negreiros, who was a nationalist in quest of Portuguese identity, received important official commissions from the Salazar government, among them the murals in the marine terminals of the port of Lisbon – literally the gateways to Portugal.

124. Pyke Koch
The Shooting Gallery, 1931

Oil on canvas
66⅞ × 51⅛in/170 × 130cm
Rotterdam Boymans Van
Beuningen (Visual Arts Library)

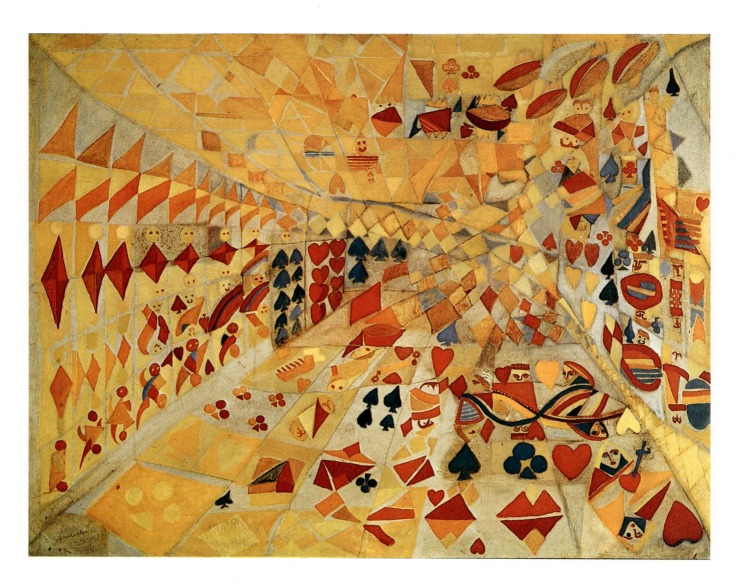

125. Maria Helena Vieira da Silva
Untitled, 1937

(Artephot/Held)

Despite the strong attraction of the Mexican muralists, Latin American art remained under European domination to a surprising extent, and here, too, there was often a strong influence from Fascist Italy as well as from France. Argentina, in any case, already had a large population of Italian rather than Spanish origin and it was logical that the Novecento should have an impact there. Lino Eneas Spilimbergo, perhaps the leading Argentine painter of the time, studied in Paris under André Lhote before returning home in 1928. There he evolved an interesting compromise between Picasso's neo-classical manner and the blander classicism prevalent in Italy.

Among the Latin American painters who reacted positively to the example of the Mexican muralists, one in particular stands out. This is the Brazilian Candido Portinari. His murals for the Brazilian Building at the New York World's Fair of 1939 differ from Mexican art not only because they are comparatively small in scale (about 10ft by 11ft;

304cm by 335cm), but because they are neither as forceful nor as crowded as Rivera's, nor are they as Expressionist as the work of Orozco and Siqueiros. Portinari is a skilful decorator, rather than a committed propagandist.

The two smaller countries that produced particularly original and distinctive work during the 1930s were Holland and Belgium. In Holland there was a well-established tradition of purist abstraction which derived from Mondrian. It still continues today. This was challenged by a new generation of realists. Among them Pyke Koch   **124** and Carel Willink. Their work falls between that of the German Magic Realists of the late 1920s — for example Franz Radziwill — and the Veristic Surrealism of Dali and Tanguy. Willink named de Chirico, Severini and Carrà among his own personal influences, and also, more surprisingly, Paul Klee. But there is also something specifically Dutch about his art in its crystal clarity and precise detail. In an eloquent essay published in 1931 Willink wrote of the way in which the Dutch painters of the twentieth century still felt themselves to be overshadowed by their great predecessors of the Golden Age. It is obvious that he himself cannot escape this heavy heritage. His *St Simeon Stylites* (1939), for all its fantasy, is a direct descendant of Jan Vermeer's seductively prosaic *View of Delft*.

In Belgium the battle was not one between abstraction and realism but one between two different styles of figuration. Belgium nurtured a strong Expressionist tradition. During the 1930s the leading Belgian painter in this style was Constant Permeke, slower and less excitable than his German equivalents, and at his best an artist capable of producing powerfully monumental images. To Permeke are opposed, in a way that reflects the division of Belgian culture between Flemish-speaking and French-speaking elements, two leading Surrealists — Paul Delvaux and René Magritte. Delvaux is Surrealist only in a somewhat   **127** marginal way. Just as Permeke owes many debts to nineteenth-century Realism, and in particular to Courbet and Daumier, so Delvaux is the heir to the turn-of-the-century Symbolist Movement, which had flourished particularly strongly in Belgium. The point is driven home when the artist clothes some of his female figures in the costumes of

205

126. René Magritte
The Rape, 1934

Oil on canvas
73 × 54.5cm
Houston, collection De Menil
(Visual Arts Library)

1900. More characteristically, however, his mysterious alienated landscapes are populated by female nudes – the emblems of a rather wan eroticism.

Magritte is a much tougher artist – the most remarkable Surrealist to have flourished away from the milieu dominated by André Breton (though Magritte did spend three years in the Parisian Surrealist group before returning to Belgium in 1930). Magritte was originally inspired by de Chirico, and it was from a study of de Chirico's *pittura metafisica* that he evolved the forthright realistic technique he used for most of his career. Whereas de Chirico eventually became embarrassed by his own bluntness of touch, and came to regard it as proof of juvenile clumsiness in handling the medium, Magritte seems to have cultivated this particular manner for its neutrality. During the 1930s he often painted like an extremely skilled and efficient sign-painter. The stern clarity and prosaic absence of mannerism that Magritte cultivated (not

for nothing was one of his favourite images that of a *petit bourgeois* figure wearing a bowler hat) are put at the service of an imagination that is simultaneously fantastic and sardonic. Magritte is a master of visual puns – a landscape painting on an easel, placed in front of a window, will exactly match the view it overlaps; or a nude female torso, crowned with flowing locks of hair, will serve as a grotesque substitute for a face. The American critic James Thrall Soby speaks of the 'rape of commonsense' that occurs in Magritte's art. 'Usually,' he adds drily, 'in broad daylight'. Though Magritte is not at all a political artist, the work he did during the 1930s, which is probably his best, sums up the pervasive feeling of unease and anxiety that characterize the decade as a whole.

127. Paul Delvaux
Pygmalion, 1939

Oil on wood
$46\frac{1}{16} \times 58\frac{1}{16}$in/117 × 147.5cm
Bruxelles Musée des Beaux Arts,
Brussels (Visual Arts Library)

126

The Fate of the Refugees

The political upheavals of the 1930s, triggered as they often were by nationalism, had the paradoxical effect of uprooting artists and sending them into exile, thus spreading stylistic influences further and faster than they might otherwise have travelled. Yet one must be careful not to claim that this uprooting was something entirely new. In the years before World War I, there had of course been a voluntary migration to Paris of artists attracted by the revolution that was taking place there. Among those who made the pilgrimage to France were Pablo Picasso, Constantin Brancusi and Amedeo Modigliani. After the war France continued to attract artists from far and wide. Some stayed for a while, then returned to their home countries; others settled permanently. For aspiring Modernists in England and America a period in France became almost as obligatory as the sojourn in Italy had been for their eighteenth- and nineteenth-century predecessors. But in the 1920s there were also exiles who had chosen France for political as well as artistic reasons, chief among them the Russians who had opted out of the Russian Revolution.

By the 1930s, those Russians who wanted to leave Russia and who had been able to find a way of doing so, had long departed. Stalin's regime kept a tight hold on its citizens and allowed them little freedom to travel. From 1933 onwards the new generation of political exiles were the refugees from Nazi Germany, and later those from an Austria forcibly united to the Third Reich by the Anschluss. Unlike the great flood of refugees who made their way to America in the 1940s, the exiles of the 1930s were fewer in number and had greater choice as to where they would settle. There were a number of European countries still open to them where they could live and work, though often on precarious terms. Understandably, the majority were reluctant to make a complete break with Europe, and many remained as close to Germany as possible. Some whom the Nazis had characterized as 'degenerate artists' could not bear to leave at all. Emil Nolde, once a member of the Nazi Party, had over a thousand works confiscated from German museums in 1937, but remained at his home in Seebull. In 1941 he was forbidden to paint, but continued to work, making small 'secret' works whose existence was revealed after the war. Ernst

128

Barlach and Käthe Kollwitz also remained in Germany, as did one of the leaders of the *Neue Sachlichkeit*, Otto Dix.

Of those who left, some had very urgent reasons for doing so. John Heartfield had used his photomontages to mount savage attacks on the Nazi leadership during the period of their rise to power. In 1933 his house was seized by the SA and he fled to Prague. Here he continued to satirize the leaders of the new Germany, seeing no need to vary a style that had already proven its effectiveness. His work stung the Nazis so much that after the Munich Agreement the Germans demanded Heartfield's extradition. The Czech government refused and Heartfield made his way to England. During the war he worked for English publishers, after being freed from a camp for enemy aliens.

Georg Grosz, once Heartfield's colleague in the Berlin Dada group, had, more than any other artist, created the public image of the Weimar Republic in all its decadence and cynicism. He too knew that a Germany ruled by the Nazis would be a dangerous place for him to be.

128. Emil Nolde
The Sea, 1930

Oil on canvas
29 × 39¾in × 73.6 × 101cm
The Tate Gallery, London (Visual Arts Library)

129

130

209

He went to America to teach in 1932, and settled there permanently in 1933. He did not benefit artistically from the change of milieu, and there is universal agreement that the work he produced in his later years lacked its former bite and conviction.

Perhaps the greatest of the German figurative painters who went into exile at this time was Max Beckmann. Nearly ten years older than Grosz, Beckmann was already a successful artist in the pre-war Expressionist milieu. He was severely shaken by his wartime experiences, and in 1915 was invalided out of the German army suffering from a nervous breakdown. Nevertheless the war and its horrors seem to have been things he was already half expecting. In 1918 he wrote: 'So the war is reaching its unhappy end, it has done nothing to change my idea of life, only confirmed it.' He made a complete break after the war, leaving his wife and moving away from Berlin. The first half of the 1920s was a period of slow convalescence, culminating in remarriage. Beckmann evolved a startling new style to convey his sense of the cruelty and futility of the world, often using carnival and circus imagery. Though his style is more fantastic than that of the 'realists' of the period, such as Dix, it is clear that he exercised a great influence over them, and that he was partly responsible for inventing the grotesque and sinister imagery that generally typifies Weimar art.

By 1925 Beckmann was already painting pictures (among them the *Galleria Umberto* of that year) which seem to predict a new holocaust. For him, the Nazi takeover, when it came, was not a startling novelty — it represented a continuation of events with which he had been intimately involved since 1914. He had for some time been pulling up his roots. From 1930 onwards he spent several months a year in Paris where he had a studio, though he deliberately kept aloof from the Parisian avant-garde. When the Nazis took power, he was forced to give up his teaching post in Frankfurt, but was still reluctant to sever all connections with Germany. He moved to Berlin, hoping to go on working there unobtrusively. His art nevertheless, however, tells us much about his state of mind. During the crucial year 1932–3 he produced the first of the series of triptychs that collectively form the crowning achievement of his career. Entitled *Departure*, it shows two

129. John Heartfield
*The Vision of Lenin Has
Become Reality*, 1934

Photomontage
$14\frac{15}{16} \times 10\frac{5}{8}$in/38 × 27cm
Berlin, Heartfield Archives (Visual
Arts Library)

scenes of torture and terror flanking a central canvas that depicts the
survivors of a new Deluge. They are in a boat on a calm sea, and among
them is a crowned figure who reinaugurates life on earth by releasing a
net load of fish into the water.

Beckmann left Germany for good after the Degenerate Art exhibition of 1937, in which he was pilloried. From then until the outbreak of
war he divided his time between Paris and Amsterdam. In 1939 he was
invited to teach at the Chicago Art Institute, but was unable to leave
Holland before being trapped there for the duration of the war by the
Nazi invasion. He spent the war years in Amsterdam, in circumstances
of considerable hardship, and finally moved to the United States in
1947, dying there in 1950.

Many of Beckmann's greatest canvases belong to his period of exile.
In 1940–1, for example, he painted another triptych, now in the

211

130. George Grosz
The Pillars of Society, 1926

Oil on canvas
$78\frac{11}{16} \times 42\frac{1}{2}$ in/200×108 cm
Berlin, National Gallery (Edimedia)

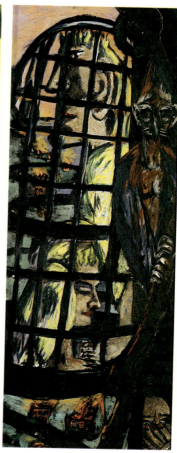

Folkwang Museum, Essen. Its theme is the legend of Perseus. The central canvas portrays the Greek hero as a brutal Nordic freebooter who is making Andromeda his prisoner, rather than setting her free. The left-hand panel shows an all-wise Buddha (the symbol of renunciation and non-violence, who is recognizable by his huge ears) in the guise of an Indonesian cook in an Amsterdam sailors' dive. Both the compression of the imagery on the canvas and its ambiguity are typical of the artist.

Though Beckmann's work was well known and widely exhibited at this time, especially in America, he remained isolated artistically throughout the period under review, and it is only now, half a century later, that one detects his widespread influence on contemporary artists. The Neo-Expressionists of the 1980s owe much to his bold yet elliptical style. He is a living presence in contemporary art, and perhaps surpasses even Picasso in this respect.

One artist whose career offers certain parallels with that of Beckmann is the Austrian Expressionist Oskar Kokoschka. Kokoschka was born in 1886, and like Beckmann he was a precocious success. He had already established an important reputation before World War I.

131. Max Beckmann
Perseus and Andromeda, 1941

Triptych, oil on canvas
central panel $59\frac{9}{16} \times 43\frac{5}{16}$in/
150×110cm
side panels $59\frac{9}{16} \times 21\frac{5}{8}$in/$150 \times 55$cm
Folkwang Museum, Essen

His stormy love affair with Alma Mahler, the widow of the composer Gustav Mahler, was just coming to its end at the time when war broke out, and Kokoschka instantly volunteered, as much to resolve a difficult personal situation as out of patriotism. In 1915 he was severely wounded in the head when fighting on the Polish front. Part of his long convalescence was spent in Dresden, and he remained in this city after the war, teaching at the Dresden Academy during the early 1920s, while trying to recover both physically and psychologically from his injuries. From 1924 to 1931 he travelled widely, then returned for a while to Vienna before settling in Prague in 1934, partly for political reasons but partly to be near his invalid sister who lived there. While in Prague he attracted the attention of the Nazis because of his friendship with Tomás Masaryk, the President of the Czechoslovak Republic. One of Kokoschka's significant paintings of this time (1935–6) is his allegorical portrait of Masaryk accompanied by the Moravian humanist Jan Amos Comenius (1592–1650), for whom the two men shared an admiration.

Kokoschka's position at this period was ambiguous. His work, like that of Beckmann and other artists, was being rooted out of German museums. He was deeply shocked both by Nazi atrocities and by the horrors of the Spanish Civil War. But he was not as yet excluded from his native Austria, and in 1937 a great Kokoschka exhibition was held in Vienna. Kokoschka himself nevertheless felt increasingly insecure even in Prague, and the 1938 Munich Agreement prompted him to move to London. But here he was unrecognized and at first almost friendless, though his reputation stood high elsewhere – between 1938 and 1945 nine Kokoschka exhibitions were held in the United States, and there were others in Switzerland and in the Netherlands. Kokoschka later recalled these years of 'humiliation and deprivation' in London with unmistakable bitterness – his production during the war years consisted largely of drawings, as he was often too poor to buy canvas and paint.

Stylistically Kokoschka was as isolated as Beckmann, and like Beckmann he turned increasingly to the art of the past. But where Beckmann drew on Late Gothic sources, Kokoschka's work, especially

his figure painting, carries strong echoes of the Austrian Baroque. He can thus be situated on the fringes of the classical revival that manifested itself so strongly elsewhere at the same epoch. One thing that linked him very definitely to the more conservative currents in the art of the period, and at the same time limited the extent of his influence, was his violent distaste for the non-figurative. Kokoschka later declared:

Non-objective art is itself the worst of all our spiritual enemies. Art without vision is hostile to life and hostile to the world. Man is the measure of all things. Whoever uses any other measure, measures falsely.

Kokoschka would presumably have included his great contemporary Kandinsky in this blanket condemnation of non-figurative art.

132. Oskar Kokoschka
Portrait of Tomás Masaryk,
1935–6

Oil on canvas
37 × 50⅜in/94 × 128cm
Museum of Art, Carnegie Institute, Pittsburgh, Pennsylvania; Museum Purchase: Patrons Art Fund, 1956

215

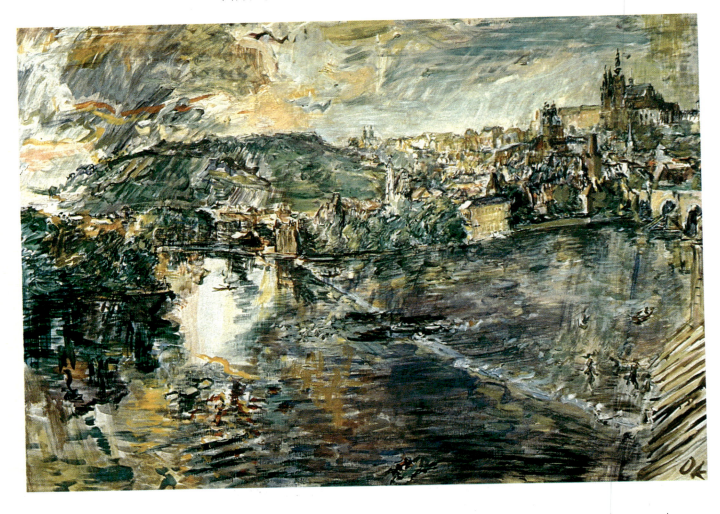

133. Oskar Kokoschka
View of Prague from the River,
1936

Oil on canvas
38 × 52in/97 × 132cm
Washington, Phillips Collection
(Visual Arts Library)

Wassily Kandinsky, who has the best claim to have invented pure abstraction, left Germany shortly after the Nazis came to power in 1933. Born in 1866, he was already well into his sixties. Though he had been born and educated in Russia, he had lived largely in Germany since 1896 – his longest period of absence was during the war years. In 1921 Kandinsky took up a teaching post at the Bauhaus, and he remained one of the most loyal servants of the Bauhaus ideal throughout the stormy life of the Weimar Republic. When the school was closed, however, he seems to have laid down his burden with something approaching a sigh of relief. In December 1933 he settled in Neuilly-sur-Seine, just outside Paris, and here he lived for the rest of his life, becoming a French citizen in 1939. His attitudes can be gauged from a letter he wrote in 1936, in reply to one from his old friend the composer Arnold Schoenberg, by this time living in America:

After I arrived here I had a wonderful feeling of freedom – external and inner – just because after fourteen years of teaching I suddenly had no more fixed obligations. My wish would be to keep it, to preserve it further, not to lose it anymore.

He added in a postscript:

Yes, it would be lovely to come to America if only for a visit. I have been planning it for years. But even apart from the not inconsiderable costs there have always been all kinds of obstacles in the way. During the first years after emigration, I didn't want to leave Paris at all, in order to enjoy and turn to account as fully as possible the freedom to work which had finally come.

Kandinsky's work underwent no dramatic or surprising developments during his final period in France. The mood of the late paintings is relaxed, and often they show traces of the quirky humour Kandinsky had learned from Paul Klee during their long association on the Bauhaus staff. In any case, their creator would have scorned to fill them with political content. Kandinsky believed firmly that 'the content of painting is painting', and that abstract art was a 'pure' form of expression directly comparable with music.

The mood in Klee's own late work is less sunny, but this was due as much to the onset of debilitating illness as it was to the artist's depression induced by the political situation. Klee had already left the Bauhaus in 1931, and had taken up a post at the Düsseldorf Academy, which the Nazis forced him to relinquish. He was a Swiss citizen, and returned to his native Berne. Klee's production from then onwards took on an increasingly bitter tone, with direct satire replacing his former playfulness. Technically he was more provocative than ever — his touch became cruder and more forceful. But this apparent crudity reveals itself on closer inspection to be a stylistic instrument of extreme flexibility. Some of the paintings and drawings Klee produced at this period show him to have been a precursor of Jean Dubuffet's post-war experiments with *Art Brut*.

The two Bauhaus-connected exiles who exercised the greatest influence in exile were both of them less celebrated as artists than Klee and Kandinsky. Their impact did not come from their work alone, but

134

135

217

from their activity as teachers. László Moholy-Nagy, born in Hungary in 1895, began teaching at the Bauhaus in 1923, succeeding Klee as head of the mural workshop and Johannes Itten in the Foundation Course. When Walter Gropius, the founder of the Bauhaus, resigned in 1928 because of the rising political pressures surrounding the institution, Moholy followed suit, and during the final years of the Weimar Republic he pursued a career as a stage designer, working for the Kroll Opera (the progressive State Opera House) and also for the great director Erwin Piscator. His interests covered a wide range – he was an abstract artist, who particularly enjoyed experimenting with new synthetic materials, an innovative layout designer and typographer, an experimental photographer and a leading exhibition designer.

Moholy always claimed to be totally non-political, but he found the situation in Germany so oppressive that he moved to Amsterdam in 1934, where he was welcomed and made the subject of a comprehensive exhibition at the Stedelijk Museum. The following year he moved again, to London. Here he continued to work on layouts and posters, and also on interior design and display. One of his clients was the Piccadilly department store, Simpson's. He was also hired by his Hungarian compatriot, the film producer Alexander Korda, to provide special effects for *Things to Come*, a film based on the novel of the same title by H. G. Wells, but these were dropped from the final print. During this brief English period, when he was in contact with the English avant-garde – among them Hepworth, Nicholson and Moore – Moholy made what were in the long term some of his most influential works: three-dimensional paintings of Plexiglas that he called 'space-modulators'.

In 1937 he made his way to Chicago, where he had been invited to set up a 'New Bauhaus'. The enterprise soon collapsed when the backers ran out of funds, but Moholy managed to continue on his own, setting up a School of Design in a disused bakery. Though beset with financial problems which restricted its activity, it survived the war years and (now renamed the Institute of Design) finally became part of the University of Chicago-Illinois. Moholy-Nagy died of leukemia in 1945.

Despite his own continuing activity as a painter, Moholy's direct

136

134. Wassily Kandinsky
N.26 Noir Bizarre, 1935

(Visual Arts Library)

influence during his later years affected design and typography more than it did fine art. In the longer term his work in America was important for artists – the relatively few people whom he had time to train became important as teachers, and they carried with them Moholy's doctrine that abstract art could fully integrate itself into American society. At the end of his life he wrote:

> The artist's duty is not to be always in opposition. He sometimes can better concentrate his forces on the central problem of visually constituting this world *in status nascendi* and only treat the shortcomings of society as transitory facts on the periphery of his efforts.

This attitude prepared the way for the reconciliation which took place during the 1950s between the American avant-garde and a wide spectrum of potential patrons.

Moholy's long-term influence was rooted not only in his own gifts, but in his ability to make reference to the system of ideas elaborated collectively at the Bauhaus during the 1920s. The same can be said of his colleague Josef Albers, whose early career was even more closely identified with this remarkable institution. Albers first entered the Bauhaus as a student, in 1920. He began doing some teaching there before the conclusion of his own apprenticeship, and in 1923 he was invited to join the staff. From 1925 he taught part of the all-important Foundation Course, the seedbed of Bauhaus ideas, and on Moholy's departure in 1928 he took over the whole of it, as well as taking charge of the furniture workshop.

On the closure of the Bauhaus in 1933 Albers and his wife Anni were invited to America, to teach at the newly founded Black Mountain College in North Carolina. Albers was to remain there until 1949 and his career as a teacher lasted until his death in 1976.

Albers first became known as an artist through his work in stained glass, made from 'found' materials – smashed bottles and other fragments of glass rescued from rubbish dumps. Thanks to the methods Albers adopted, these glass collages have an irregularity that bring them close to certain kinds of 'free' abstraction produced in the

137

135. Paul Klee
Facial Expression, 1939

$23\frac{5}{8} \times 17\frac{9}{16}$ in/60 × 44.7cm
Zurich Kunsthaus (Visual Arts Library)

221

136. László Moholy-Nagy
Light-Space Modulator, 1931
reconstructed in 1970

Mobile construction with steel,
plastic and wood
59½in/151.1cm high with base
(Visual Arts Library)

years that immediately followed World War II. Klee admired what the young Albers was doing and encouraged him to exhibit his work, but Albers did not make a major name as a creative artist, either then, or for many years to come. His reputation as a creator of the first rank only burgeoned with the *Homage to the Square* series, the first of which was painted as late as 1950. Apparently very different from Albers's earlier work in glass, the *Homage to the Square* paintings have a subterranean link with the earlier collages. Both are demonstrations of ideas that Albers put forward to his pupils throughout his long

222

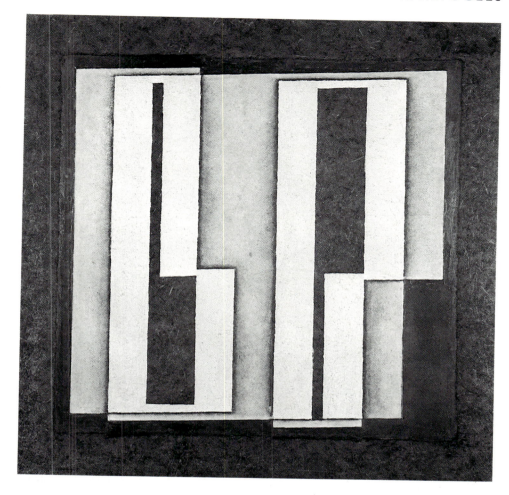

137. Josef Albers
b. and p., 1937

Oil on Masonite
$23\frac{7}{8} \times 23\frac{3}{4}$in/60.6 × 60.3cm
Solomon R. Guggenheim Museum,
New York (photo Carmelo
Guadagno)

career as a teacher. The chief of these was that the fundamental step in becoming an artist was not learning how to make but learning how to see.

In a real sense Albers brought this concept to the Bauhaus, rather than finding it waiting for him. His predecessors in shaping the Foundation Course, Itten and especially Moholy-Nagy, put much greater emphasis on the production of finished objects. By taking the concept to the United States, Albers exercised a profound influence over the future of American art and indeed over that of modern art in general.

There was one German émigré not connected to the Bauhaus who exercised an important influence in America. This was Hans Hofmann. Like Albers, Hofmann arrived in the United States with an established reputation as a teacher. He had run a school of his own in Munich which was well regarded, and summer schools in Ragusa, Capri and Saint-Tropez. His decision to settle on the other side of the Atlantic was not directly precipitated by political events. Hofmann first taught

138

in America at the Chouinard Art Institute, Los Angeles, and the University of California, Berkeley, during 1930. In 1932–3 he taught at the Art Students' League in New York, and at a school in Gloucester, Massachusetts. Subsequently he ran his own schools of art in New York and Provincetown Massachusetts.

His exhibition record until his show at Peggy Guggenheim's Art of This Century Gallery in 1944 (the breeding ground of Abstract Expressionism) is extremely sparse. There was a show at the Paul Cassirer Gallery, Berlin, in 1910; one at the California Palace of the Legion of Honor, San Francisco, in 1931; and one in New Orleans in 1940. Hofmann remained a not very distinguished figurative Expressionist until the beginning of the 1940s. During this period his importance for American art lay neither in his personal achievement nor in his promotion of one central idea but in his function as a catalyst – a focal point for the aspirations of American colleagues who were feeling their way towards something new, and a source of information about the European art-world. Hofmann had studied at the École de la Grande Chaumière in Paris at the same time as Matisse, and had been a friend of Robert Delaunay. Even more important was the fact that Hofmann was equipped, both by temperament and by background, to re-enact Kandinsky's shift from figurative Expressionism to something fluidly and freely abstract. Witnessing this change in someone they already respected highly was very important for his American associates. The thing Hofmann brought to American painting was a growing trust in improvisation which the Bauhaus-connected exiles, more intellectual, more systematic and still deeply rooted in European Constructivism were not in a position to inculcate. Nevertheless, the main drama of Hofmann's 'conversion' took place after the 1930s had come to a close, and therefore has only a marginal place in this book.

138. Hans Hofmann
Still Life – Yellow Table on Green, 1936

Oil on board
60 × 44½in/152.4 × 113cm
Andre Emmerich Gallery (Visual Arts Library)

American Abstract Art

At first sight, American art in the 1930s largely represents a reaction against what had happened in the 1920s, with few positive values of its own. This impression is erroneous. During the decade important foundations were built. Without these, American art could not have enjoyed the dominant position it achieved post-1940.

In America, the 1920s were a period of stylistic experiment. This followed in the wake of the Armory Show of 1913, which formally introduced the American audiences to Modernism and its possibilities. The Armory Show helped and harmed the American avant-garde. American artists were of course included, but their work was almost overlooked in the midst of all the excitement generated by their European colleagues. Significantly, much of the attention went to minor rather than major Cubists – Francis Picabia, Marcel Duchamp and Albert Gleizes, rather than to Georges Braque and Pablo Picasso.

139 Duchamp's *Nude Descending a Staircase* (1912) was the single most-discussed work. One reason why the media focused on these artists rather than on others was that all three of them were present in person at about the time of the exhibition.

Post-1920, Abstraction and Cubism remained of intense interest to ambitious American artists, especially those who took the New York art-world as their focus. But the styles used in the 1920s and 1930s passed into oblivion with the advent of Abstract Expressionism – this applied even to the early efforts of the leading Abstract Expressionists, who had often practised art for many years before they made their breakthrough into a new style. It has taken strenuous efforts on the part of scholars and curators to resurrect the experimental art of the period, at least in part. Even in its own day the abstract art of the 1930s had to meet a number of difficult challenges, among them the accusation that it was slavishly dependent on Europe, and perhaps more damaging, that its practitioners lived in an ivory tower and were indifferent to the economic consequences of the Slump. But there were also institutions and individuals who made it a policy to defend this kind of artistic creativity, though sometimes they did so in an ambiguous way. The chief disseminator of information about Modernism in the visual arts was undoubtedly New York's Museum of Modern

226

139. Marcel Duchamp
*Nude Descending a Staircase
No.* 2, 1912

Oil on canvas
57 × 35in/147 × 89cm
Philadelphia Museum of Art:
Walter & Louise Arensberg
Collection

Art, which opened its doors to the public in 1929. One of its most influential exhibitions was 'Cubism and Modern Art', put on by Alfred Barr in 1936. This presented the abstract art of the early twentieth century as a continuous, logical process of evolution. At the same time, however, the Museum, by its omission of all American artists from the show with the sole exception of Alexander Calder, seemed to express the view that art in America would more fruitfully pursue a different path, directed towards realism.

A different assessment had been presented to the New York public the year before, by another new institution, the Whitney Museum of American Art. 'Abstract Painting in America' was a complete panorama of American activity in this field from the Armory Show until the mid-1930s. It contained 134 works by most of the leading artists associated with abstraction.

The catalogue introduction to the Whitney exhibition was written by Stuart Davis (1894–1964), then undoubtedly the most original and influential post-Cubist painter in America. Davis had pioneered a return to abstraction in the 'Eggbeater' series of 1927–8 (now also regarded as precursors of Pop Art, because of their use of banal mass-manufactured objects). He had then spent a year and a half in Paris before returning to New York in August 1929. The work he did in the first half of the 1930s is a true synthesis of French and American preoccupations. He made a series of views of the waterfront at Gloucester, Massachusetts – the kind of subject-matter beloved by the American Scene artists who were the abstractionists' greatest rivals, infusing them with the jazzy rhythms of contemporary American life, and also with some of the dryness of the Puritan New England past. But the idiom he used was nevertheless a version of Cubism – indebted to Léger and to certain Picassos of the late 1920s, which he must have seen during his visit to Paris.

As well as being an original and greatly gifted artist, Davis was a strong personality and a good organizer. In the mid-1930s he became more and more of a public figure. In 1934 he was elected to the presidency of the newly founded Artists' Union; and in 1938 he became Chairman of the American Artists' Congress. At this period he was an eloquent spokesman for the view that Modernist art could also possess a social conscience. He also became heavily involved in various federal art programmes, both as an organizer and, creatively, as a painter of murals – he was not immune to the enthusiasm for these which swept the American art-world during the decade, though he was never tempted to imitate the Mexicans stylistically. His best mural, *Swing Landscape* (1938), painted for the Williamsburg Housing Project, and now in the Indiana University Art Museum, Bloomington, is an extremely accomplished essay in Léger's idiom, with a particular debt to the latter's *La Ville* of 1919. Nevertheless, for Davis the second half of the decade was a period of mounting disillusionment with the Stalinist Left, and his disaffection reached a head with the Stalinist takeover of the American Artists' Congress in 1940. His subsequent abandonment of public life was accompanied by an at least partial abandonment of his insistence that all subject-matter must be rooted

140

in common experience. Yet all his paintings retained at least an analogical relationship to the natural world. And though Davis continued to predict the end of the European hegemony in American art, he himself was never entirely free of it, and this compromised his claim to be the true leader of the American vanguard when the revolution initiated in the 1940s began to gain impetus.

Though Davis now seems not only the best American abstractionist of the period but the one whose work is most typically American, despite its incorporation of foreign influences, he remained comparatively isolated. 'Typical' American abstraction in the 1930s was geometrical and non-figurative. Its debts were to the Bauhaus, the Constructivism of Gabo and Pevsner, the Neo-Plasticism of Mondrian, and sometimes even to the Suprematism of Malevich. Mondrian in particular exercised a significant influence over American artists long before his arrival in New York in 1940, and many of them contrived to meet him in Paris. Among the leading American non-objectivists were Charles Biedermann, Ilya Bolotowsky, Burgoyne Diller and Jean Xceron, many of these spending long periods abroad, studying and perfecting their craft. At home, a number of them enjoyed the patronage and encouragement of Solomon R. Guggenheim, and his formidable curator and adviser Baroness Hilla Rebay, though few agreed with Rebay's mystical interpretation of the purposes of abstract art. Their careers were often far more picturesque and romantic than their paintings.

140. Stuart Davis
Swing Landscape, 1938

Oil on canvas
$86\frac{11}{16} \times 172\frac{7}{8}$in/220.3 × 439.2cm
Indiana University Art Museum,
Bloomington

A case in point is Jean Xceron (1890–1967). He was born in a remote Greek mountain village, and arrived in America at the age of fourteen. During his early years in the United States he earned his living in a variety of humble jobs – cleaning hats, working as a shoeshine boy, selling ice-creams and candy. In 1910 he settled in Washington and began to study at the Corcoran School of Art, which he attended intermittently until 1917. In Washington he was introduced simultaneously to the tradition of classical antiquity (through the museum casts he was required to copy), and to the doctrines of Modernism (through his fellow students). In 1920 he moved to New York, where he had further contact with the avant-garde, and by 1927 he had at last saved enough money to go to Paris. There Joáquin Torres-García, already a friend and mentor from New York days, introduced him to Theo van Doesburg, Mondrian, Jean Hélion, Léger and Arp. Xceron's work at this time still retained traces of figuration, but these vanished soon after his temporary return to New York in 1935 for an exhibition of his work at the Garland Gallery, New York. On this occasion Xceron found himself much sought after by younger artists as someone who could report at first hand on the situation in Europe. The great flood of European refugees had not as yet begun.

In 1938, Xceron once more settled permanently in New York, beginning a long association with Rebay and the Solomon R. Guggenheim Foundation.

He is a good example of two things – first, of the long struggle many artists of his generation endured in order to reach the point where they could think of calling themselves professionals; and second, of the way in which a whole generation of American abstract artists, apparently well established after the struggles of the 1930s, went into eclipse with the rise of Abstract Expressionism. It is significant that Xceron did not exhibit for five years after a show held in 1950 at the Sidney Janis Gallery, and that when he started exhibiting his work again he found himself totally cut off from the new mainstream of American art.

The artists we now think of as the major masters of the new style of the 1940s and 1950s were most of them already at work in the 1930s. In

141. Jackson Pollock
Self-Portrait, 1933

Oil on canvas
Marlborough Gallery Inc, New
York (Visual Arts Library)

141

142

some cases – Jackson Pollock is an example – what they produced then was far removed from what they were to do later. In another case, the artist concerned took considerable pains to cover his own tracks. Barnett Newman, though a practising painter throughout the decade, destroyed all his own work previous to 1944.

The transitional figures in the creation of a new aesthetic were John Graham (1886–1961) and Arshile Gorky (1904–48), though Graham was much more important as a catalyst and conduit of ideas than for his own work as a painter – during the 1930s he produced extremely accomplished versions of Picasso, and later he was to turn towards a kind of rhetorical classicism. He exerted influence through his wide knowledge of art, fascinating personality and genius for friendship. Graham's history was even more extraordinary than Jean Xceron's. Born Ivan Gratianovitch Dombrowski (or Dabrovsky) he was of aristocratic Polish origin, and as a young man had moved in the orbit of the Imperial Russian Court. At the time of the Revolution he sided with the Whites, and narrowly escaped execution by the Bolsheviks for counter-revolutionary activity. He made his way to America, and

231

142. Arshile Gorky
Painting, 1936–7

Oil on canvas
38 × 48in/96.5 × 122cm
Whitney Museum, New York

there art, formerly a hobby, became an obsession. In the early 1920s he studied at the Art Students' League in New York, and then settled in Baltimore, where he was befriended by Duncan Phillips, creator of the great Phillips Collection in Washington. Finding it hard to earn a living from his art, Graham became a successful art-dealer, specializing in Italian Renaissance bronzes and ethnographical objects. His range of friendships expanded to include Stuart Davis, Willem de Kooning, David Smith and Arshile Gorky. These four names are an index of his perceptiveness, as well as of Graham's own personal allure.

Gorky's early life was as exotic and violent as Graham's, though he was considerably younger. He had arrived in America in 1920 at the age of sixteen, after barely surviving the massacre of the Armenians in Turkey. His name, like Graham's, was assumed. Born Vosdanig

Manoog Adoian, he became Arshile Gorky in 1925, and even went so far as to pretend that he was a cousin of the celebrated Russian writer. His talent as a painter was recognized early by his peers, but they were baffled by its peculiarity – Gorky seemed to have an obsessional need to recapitulate all the major styles of Modernism in his own work. Picasso in particular mesmerized him, but he also painted versions of Cézanne, Léger, Miró and Kandinsky.

As the decade progressed Gorky's derivativeness became less marked, but it was not until the mid-1940s that he liberated himself completely from his exemplars, and went on to achieve the mature style on which his reputation now rests. Yet Gorky's apparent pastiches often possess a quality denied to other American abstract art of the period – intensity. His power of empathy gives some of his early pictures and drawings memorable force.

Among the throng of other artists who formed part of the New York milieu, two are especially worthy of notice. One is the sculptor David Smith. Smith is now so closely identified with the art produced during a very prolific period at the end of his life that it is not generally realized how early he matured. He studied during the late 1920s at the Art Students' League, intending at first to be a painter – indeed he later claimed, at least half seriously, that he still belonged with the painters rather than with the sculptors. But, while he was still a student, he started to turn his paintings into reliefs, and eventually into three-dimensional constructions. An important turning point came when John Graham showed him pictures of welded metal sculptures by Picasso and Julio González in the magazine *Cahiers d'Art*, and Smith realized that the techniques he had learned while working as a welder in an automobile factory could also be used to make art.

Though his techniques increasingly came from American industry, Smith was always emphatic that his influences were European – he himself cited González, Kandinsky, Mondrian and the Cubists, and it is possible to add many other names, for example those of Giacometti and Miró. Giacometti's construction *The Palace at 4 a.m.* clearly **92** provided the American artist with the inspiration for his *Interior for Exterior* of 1939, which is in fact a kind of paraphrase. But unlike Gorky,

Smith manages to escape the trap of imitation. He always preserves an independent relationship to his models. One original aspect of his art is his use of sculpture to make statements about landscape – a number of pieces from this period are landscapes 'drawn' in metal (rather than the figure-as-landscape associated with Henry Moore). Even more original was Smith's insouciant ad hocism. He was already beginning to extend the collage principle and to incorporate all kinds of found objects in his work. A pair of pliers features in *Interior for Exterior*. These collage elements owe a debt to Analytic Cubism, and to Picasso's later transformations of found objects, but they are also different in spirit – not changed by their context but simply swallowed up by it. Picasso puns self-consciously, calling attention to the ambiguity of his *trouvailles*. David Smith, by contrast, is simply a man who makes use of whatever an industrial civilization puts in his way.

The sculptures Smith made in the late 1930s foreshadow many of the things that would happen to American art in the late 1950s and early 1960s. He is his own ancestor, and also the ancestor of artists like Jasper Johns and Robert Rauschenberg.

My final subject demonstrates something quite different – a hidden continuity within American abstraction despite the eventual sea change that overtook European ideas when they were exposed to a different culture. Ad Reinhardt was born in 1913, and attended two art schools after graduating from Columbia University, where he played a considerable part in radical campus politics. The young Reinhardt was a 'joiner', with excellent connections. He was a member of the American Abstract Artists' Group, and was affiliated to the Artists' Union and the American Artists' Congress. Stuart Davis regarded him as a protégé, and he was employed as an easel-painter by the WPA Federal Art Project on the recommendation of Burgoyne Diller. This provided him with financial support from 1936 to 1941.

Surviving early paintings by Reinhardt show him to have been an absolutely orthodox non-objective painter of the period, using flat, brightly coloured geometric shapes with a slightly Deco look to them. They are interesting less for their own sake than because they provided a basis for the severely minimal canvases for which the artist later became celebrated. The materials are there and only need to be refined further. In the 1950s Reinhardt was to be identified, both by critics and to some extent by himself, with the now triumphant Abstract Expressionists, but his relationship to them was strange: he was the perpetual voice of opposition within their ranks. In 1955 he published a manifesto against Abstract Expressionist rhetoric. 'Painting,' he wrote, 'is special, separate, a matter of meditation and contemplation, for me, no physical action or social sport.' He can be regarded as the most important link between the New York Constructivism of the 1930s, with which he grew up, and the Minimal Art just coming to prominence at the time of his death in 1967.

This account of the New York art-scene during the 1930s necessarily omits many of the issues that seemed desperately important at the time – the fight against Fascism, the struggle between various shades of left-wing opinion (despite the presence of certain 'gentlemen artists', such as A. E. Gallatin, George Morris and Charles Shaw, most of the New York art community inclined towards the left). What it tries to do is to give some idea of the growing points for the new American art that was to emerge within the next two decades. The New York Abstractionists, looking towards Europe for their values, were being challenged throughout the decade, and for the most part it seemed successfully, by artists who espoused a very different set of values. The 1930s were an epoch when painters and sculptors consciously tried to explore the idea of what it was to be American. They were also an epoch of unprecedented government intervention into the affairs of artists. Both the artists' own explorations and their dialogue with the federal government seemed to lead them, not towards abstraction, and certainly not towards versions or paraphrases of European styles, but towards an indigenous kind of realism. Even so, there remained several ways in which the notion of realism could be interpreted.

Social Realism in America

Many artists, in the America of the period, were dogmatic not only in their support of realism, but also of the much narrower idea that America itself must be the true subject of American art. Chief among them was Thomas Hart Benton, leader of the Regionalists. Benton was a man in strident reaction both against Europe itself and the modern style associated with Europe. 'I wallowed in every cockeyed -ism that came along,' he said to a friendly critic, 'and it took me ten years to get all that Modernist dirt out of my system.'

In 1930 Benton was commissioned to paint a series of murals for the New School for Social Research in New York — an equivalent, though less ambitious, commission to those Rivera was receiving in the United States at the same time. It provided Benton with the kind of opportunity he had long been seeking to make a public statement about American life. By this time, he had passed, not only through Modernism but also through a phase of left-wing radicalism — ironically, leftist political views were now taken up by many of the non-objective artists whom he detested. Yet, despite the fact that he had renounced Marxist political views, Benton's murals at the New School for Social Research still show a strong degree of influence from the leading Mexicans. It is thanks to them, for example, that the compositions show a lingering hint of Cubism, with figures forced into compartments too small for them, and looming forms pressed close against the picture plane. Every detail is deliberately energized, in response to the painter's conviction that energy was the hallmark of American life. At the same time he makes use of devices that come, not from high art, but from mass culture. The surface of the painting is segmented to provide a multitude of different vignettes, in a way that recalls the tabloid sections of contemporary newspapers.

The early 1930s brought Benton a number of important commissions for murals. The earlier ones were in New York — first those at the New School for Social Research, then another set for the library of the Whitney Museum. They made Benton an extremely controversial figure in the New York art-world — he was much attacked and responded pugnaciously. His New York murals were followed in turn by two major commissions in the Midwest — a series of paintings for the

145

143. Philip Evergood
Dance Marathon, 1934

Huntington Art Gallery, the University of Texas at Austin (James and Mari Michener Collection)

144. William Gropper
The Senate, 1935

Oil on canvas
$25\frac{1}{8} \times 33\frac{1}{8}$in/$63.8 \times 84.1$cm
The Museum of Modern Art, New
York. Gift of A. Conger Goodyear

State of Indiana Pavilion at the Century of Progress International Exposition held in Chicago in 1933–4, and a series for the Missouri State Capitol in Jefferson City, commissioned in 1935. In order to accept the Jefferson City commission, Benton abandoned what had become increasingly difficult negotiations concerning a mural for the new Post Office Building in Washington DC. He also decided to shake the dust of New York from his feet, settling permanently in the Midwest, where he became director of painting at the Kansas City Art Institute.

One strange aspect of Benton's career is that he never in fact executed a mural in connection with any federally funded project. The arbortive commission for the Post Office Building in Washington was the nearest he ever came to such a task, though he did advise and encourage the programme which was a major part of the Public Works of Art Project (PWAP), started in 1933.

Throughout the 1930s Benton was executing easel-paintings as well as murals. These cover a wide range. Some are studies of particular places, where Benton gave intimate expression to his feelings for the American land. But others, despite Benton's assertive nationalism, carry strong overtones from the European art movements of the time – Surrealism in some cases, the *Neue Sachlichkeit* in others. Overall, there is a baroque restlessness about most of Benton's compositions that prevents him from being a realist in the most literal sense, and

tends to link him to other figurative painters of the period – Paul Cadmus for example – whose declared aims were very different from his own.

Benton's most distinguished rival among the Regionalists, or 'American Scene' painters as they were also called, was a quieter and less deliberately controversial figure – Grant Wood. Nevertheless it was Wood, rather than Benton, who was responsible for creating the image by which the Regionalists are best remembered today. *American Gothic*, painted in 1930, just as Benton's New School murals were being created, has been parodied almost as often as the *Mona Lisa*. It still remains a powerful icon – a summary of the attitudes and values of Midwestern pioneers. Its ambiguity – is it a satire or a celebration? – is part of its enduring appeal. On the whole, Wood's attitude was celebratory. His crisp, definite, slightly archaistic style reflects his enthusiasm for American folk art, and his paintings of people also show his fascination with nineteenth-century daguerreotypes. At the heart of what he produced lies the American agrarian myth, itself the

145. Thomas Hart Benton
City Activities with Dance Hall, 1930

Mural for the New School for Social Research, New York (Edimedia)

146

239

240

product of generations of effort spent taming the prairie and creating a culture where none had previously existed.

There is a distinction to be made between Regionalist painting as it was practised by Benton, Grant Wood, and a number of other artists, and the Social Realism of the same period, which was critical rather than celebratory, and whose focus was urban rather than rural. Social Realism endured longer than Regionalism – it possessed distinguished representatives still actively at work in the 1950s and even in the 1960s, but its stylistic coherence was less marked, and its true significance is therefore harder to assess.

In the 1930s, the two most discussed Social Realist artists in America were Philip Evergood and William Gropper. They came from strikingly different backgrounds, though both were of Jewish origin. Evergood's parents were prosperous – his father was an Australian from an orthodox background, and had become a painter against his own parents' wishes; his mother was a wealthy and well-connected Englishwoman. Evergood was educated at Eton and Cambridge, and later studied art in England (at the Slade, under the high priest of drawing Henry Tonks, who formed so many English artists, among them Stanley Spencer); then in New York at the Art Students' League and in Paris under André Lhote. He was afterwards to say: 'In my youth I fled from the chance to live securely, prosperously and dully, under most propitious auspices, in order to live more agreeably though precariously as an artist.'

Gropper came from an exceedingly poor background on New York's Lower East Side. In his childhood the family were supported by his mother, who worked as a seamstress in a sweatshop. Gropper too was forced into a sweatshop, then after a brief spell on a scholarship at the National Academy of Design (they threw him out after only two weeks), he worked at a variety of menial jobs – in a clothing store, as a timekeeper on a railroad in Cuba, and as a dishwasher. His initial impact was made as a caricaturist. He worked for prosperous and conservative publications for money, and for the radical press largely for free. His reputation as a 'serious' artist was made very rapidly with a handful of murals, and with an exhibition of paintings held in 1936 at a

146. Grant Wood
American Gothic, 1930

Oil on beaver-board
$29\frac{7}{8} \times 24\frac{7}{8}$ in/76 × 63.5cm
Courtesy of the Art Institute of Chicago; Friends of the American Art Collection (Visual Arts Library)

241

147. Charles Sheeler
Rolling Power, 1939

Oil on canvas
15 × 30in/38.1 × 76.2cm
Smith College Museum of Art,
Northampton, USA

small downtown gallery in New York, which caught the fancy of critics and patrons alike.

Despite the difference in their backgrounds, Evergood and Gropper also had much in common. Both were men of the Left, who used art as a political weapon, and both can be loosely classified as Expressionists. Of the two, Evergood is the less intense. A critic remarked, of his Whitney Museum retrospective in 1960, that Evergood's painting is 'anecdotal and occasional, and therefore it is rewarding to see a lot of it at once.' This is a backhanded compliment, since it implies that he was incapable of producing a picture that would sum up all his qualities in a single statement. To some extent this is true. Many paintings seem

143 rather diffuse. Yet there are partial exceptions. *Dance Marathon*, painted in 1934 and recording a craze of the time, has a cold grotesquerie that makes Evergood seem like a lesser Max Beckmann.

Unlike Evergood, Gropper is no colourist. His training as a caricaturist gave him, in compensation, a powerful, almost sculptural sense of form. Yet when one compares him to Daumier, another great satirical draughtsman turned painter, one is aware of something missing. Gropper cannot make the medium work for him as Daumier does – there is always something a little too cut-and-dried about his

144 forms. As a result his painting *The Senate* (1935) amounts to little more than a skilful cartoon in paint.

A very different idea of America is given by the work of a group of painters who were most of them somewhat senior to Evergood and

242

Gropper, and therefore less directly the artistic offspring of the Depression. The Precisionists had begun to depict industrial subject-matter in the 1920s, using a tight, flat, stringently disciplined style influenced by Cubism on the one hand and by photography on the other. Many of the most celebrated Precisionist images, such as Charles Sheeler's *Rolling Power* of 1939, were based upon photographs. **147** Sheeler, equally skilled as a painter and a photographer, and equally committed to both media as a means of artistic expression, was already well established by the time the decade opened — he had been one of the American exhibitors at the Armory Show of 1913. His prestige remained high throughout the 1930s, and the Museum of Modern Art gave him a major retrospective in 1939.

More closely identified with the decade — and also considerably younger (he was born in 1906 whereas Sheeler was born in 1883) — was Ralston Crawford, who made industrial scenes his speciality. Depopulated, often showing only details of buildings, his paintings were built up of large, flat-colour shapes, with most details refined away. The effect is a little like the work of his British contemporary Edward Wadsworth, though Ralston is more consistent in style and also lacks Wadsworth's touch of Surrealism.

Associated at one time with the Precisionists, though never completely at one with them, was Georgia O'Keeffe. Much of her early **148** work was abstract, though always using forms rooted in the study of nature. During the 1920s, she painted a series of views of New York skyscrapers, which were her nearest approach to the work of the other painters in the Precisionist group, and in 1929 she moved to live permanently in New Mexico. During the dry summers she began to paint the animal bones she found lying about:

And as I was working I thought of the city men I had been seeing in the East. They talked so often of writing the Great American Novel — the Great American Play — the Great American Poetry. I am not sure they aspired to the Great American Painting. Cézanne was so much in the air that the Great American Painting didn't even seem a possible dream . . . I was quite excited over our country and I knew

243

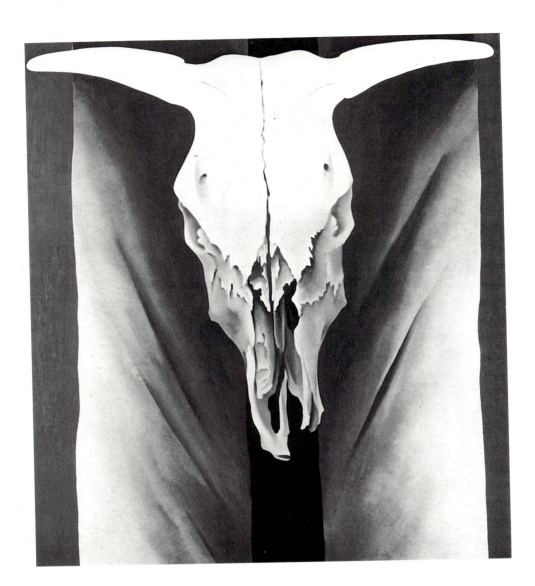

148. Georgia O'Keeffe
*Cow's Skull, Red, White and
Blue*, 1931

Oil on canvas
40 × 36in/101.6 × 91.4cm
The Metropolitan Museum of Art,
New York (Visual Arts Library)

that at that time almost any one of those great minds would have been living in Europe had it been possible for them. They didn't even want to live in New York – how was the Great American Thing going to happen? So as I painted along on my cow's skull on blue I thought to myself, 'I'll make it an American painting. They will not think it great with the red stripes down the sides – Red, White and Blue – but they will notice it.'

O'Keeffe was not the only American artist to withdraw from the urban centres. New Mexico was the choice of a number of other painters and sculptors during the inter-war years. Some, like John Marin, spent summers in the Southwest, while others settled permanently. Among the settlers were Andrew Dasburg, who after a long association with the region rooted himself there in 1933, Raymond Jonson and Maynard Dixon. Dasburg applied lessons learned from

244

Cézanne to the New Mexican landscape (thus confirming Georgia
O'Keeffe's description of the situation). Jonson and Dixon were
affected by an impulse, shared with many other artists living in and
around Santa Fé and Taos, to try and assimilate ideas from Navajo
culture. The results, in their case as in others, were rather superficial.
In his *Southwest Arrangement* of 1933 Jonson tried to make use of
patterns borrowed from Indian blankets. Dixon's figurative *Earth
Knower* of 1932–5 strains to provide an image of Indian wisdom, in an
idiom that owes much to Gauguin's paintings of Tahiti.

    Earth Knower makes a striking contrast, both in style and atmo-
sphere, with the work of an urban realist such as Paul Cadmus, and the
comparison supplies further proof of the large number of options open
to the figurative artists of the period. Cadmus is an interesting figure
for other reasons as well. At first glance, and knowing only some of his
paintings, it would be tempting to classify him as another Social Realist

149. Maynard Dixon
Earth Knower, 1932–5

Oil on canvas
40 × 50in/101.6 × 127cm
Bequest of Abilio Reis, Oakland
Museum

149

— as someone whose work is related to that of Philip Evergood. Cadmus, at this period, claimed to think of himself as a satirist above all. He said, in a catalogue introduction written in 1937:

> This, then, is my viewpoint — a satirical viewpoint; and I think I'm correct in saying that genuine satire has always been considered supremely moral. But, strangely enough, though the artistic expression is often composed of elements repulsive to the artist, the very efficacy of these repulsive and perhaps immoral elements in strengthening and achieving better social standards is a source of infinite concern and even delight to the satirical artist.
>
> Particular people, people molded by their environment and contacts, the actions of these people not only as expressions of their own nature but as products of their attempt to conciliate and ameliorate this environment: these are of the utmost concern to me. A generalized satirical concept seems to me to be less significant as art and much less effective as propaganda for correcting evils.

But there is another side to Cadmus's work — his self-consciousness about style. The satirical paintings of the 1930s, most notably a striking series devoted to the theme of sailors on the spree, show numerous references to the work of the Old Masters, for instance to the work of Luca Signorelli, whose contorted, athletic nudes Cadmus particularly **150** admired. One or two works of the period, such as *Gilding the Acrobats* of 1935, are devoid of social content, and here the mannerist element to be found in all Cadmus's work appears even more clearly.

Cadmus's liking for complex poses and exaggerated gestures links him not to the Social Realists but to Benton. These trademarks are conspicuously absent from the art of Edward Hopper, who has gradually come to be recognized as the greatest of all the realist painters of the period working in America. Hopper's mature style crystallized during the 1920s. Perhaps his earliest fully mature painting is *The House by the Railroad* of 1925. The picture combines past and present — the house belongs to the nineteenth century; the railroad suggests an inexorable movement towards the future. The starkness of the composition seems to hint at qualities deeply rooted in the

American experience: a harsh melancholy, an inexplicable sense of abandonment. In the late 1920s Hopper gradually developed both a range of subject-matter peculiar to himself and an original vision. He depicted deserted cityscapes, scenes in office and hotel lobbies, and even one or two subjects previously considered unpaintable, such as country gas stations. Everything speaks of impermanence, of the restless movement of people throughout, of the vastness of the continent — the message is therefore very different from that contained in Benton's work, though Hopper can claim to be even more identifiably 'American'. The paintings are like frames from a Hollywood film, enigmatic fragments from a narrative whose beginning and end the spectator will never be allowed to know. To compare Hopper with the German artists of the *Neue Sachlichkeit* is to perceive a vast difference as well as a superficial similarity. He is not interested in satire, or even in social commentary. He uses the deliberately familiar and ordinary to express the *lacrimae rerum*, the 'tears of things'. As a result it is he, among all his contemporaries, who most successfully conjures up the atmosphere of the period in the United States. If we want to know what the 1930s felt like, as well as what they looked like in American terms, we turn to the body of Hopper's work.

Though the abstract art of the period supplied most of the growing points for American painting and sculpture after World War II, it is the figurative work that, in retrospect, seems central. The American realists produced art that conveys a remarkably intense and truthful vision of the land they inhabited. National self-consciousness was in any case typical of the time. Mexican Muralism was founded on it; we catch more than glimpses of its darker side in the work produced in Nazi Germany, Fascist Italy, and Stalinist Russia, and there are definite traces of it in English Neo-Romanticism. Perhaps only France, as the citadel of Modernism, remained immune.

Patronage of the Arts in America

One aspect of the American art of the 1930s was so remarkable that it deserves a brief final chapter to itself. Worldwide, one of the deepest divisions in the art of the period was between public and private statements. The decade saw a considerable revival in public patronage, but this was mostly in the hands of the dictators. Public art flourished in Germany, Russia and Italy, while it languished in Britain and France. Even Mexico, though not precisely a dictatorship along Fascist or Stalinist lines, was a one-party state, and here public patronage was given added impetus by a rising tide of nationalism.

The one great democracy that experimented with public patronage on a large scale was the United States. This seems the more surprising since America is now, fifty years later, a country where there is less government intervention in the arts than one usually discovers elsewhere. Great public patrons exist, but they are large corporations, rather than government itself. During the 1930s government patronage of the visual arts took two forms. One was the direct commissioning of artists; the other was support for artists through the Works Project Administration, whose broad aim was to alleviate the worst effects of the Depression throughout American society. At first, however, the motive was in each case the same. The initial impulse seems to have been supplied by the painter George Biddle, a long-time friend of President Roosevelt. Biddle was the driving force behind the Public Works of Art Project, which was the first experimental step. The PWAP only lasted for six months, and just before it was liquidated Biddle said: 'For the first time in our history the Federal government has recognized that it has the same obligation to keep an artist alive during the depression as to keep a farmer or carpenter alive; but also that art itself is a necessary function of our social life, and must be fostered during the depression at all times. Like education, science, or hospital service, it is vested with public interest.'

The PWAP was inspired by the example already set by the Mexicans, cited by Biddle in a letter written to Roosevelt in May 1933:

The Mexican artists have produced the greatest national school mural painting since the Italian Renaissance. Diego Rivera tells me it was only possible because Obregón allowed Mexican artists to work

150. Paul Cadmus
Gilding the Acrobats, 1935

Tempera and oil on masonite
$36\frac{3}{4} \times 18\frac{1}{2}$in/93.3 × 47cm
The Metropolitan Museum of Art,
Arthur H. Hearn Fund, 1950

at a plumber's wages in order to express on the walls of the government buildings the social ideals of the Mexican revolution. The younger artists of America are conscious as they have never been of the social revolution that our country and civilization are going through; and they would be very eager to express these ideals in a permanent form if they were given the government's coopera- tion. They would be contributing to and expressing in living monuments the social ideals that you are struggling to achieve. And I am convinced that our mural art with a little impetus can soon result, for the first time in our history, in a vital national expression.

Though the PWAP only lasted six months in its original form, its success ensured that a second and related project was established only three months after its demise. In October 1934, the government created the Section of Painting and Sculpture of the Treasury Department, later called the Section of Fine Arts. In this the emphasis was switched from relief work for artists to the provision of suitable murals and sculptures for new Federal government buildings. Slightly later, the Treasury Relief Art Project was created which employed artists to provide works of art for existing buildings.

Post offices, often in remote rural areas where people had little or no contact with modern art, were particularly favoured sites for these government-commissioned murals. More than a thousand of them were created, in a wide variety of figurative styles. In many ways the programme was almost ideally democratic – the authorities invited a dialogue between themselves, the artists who were commissioned, and the communities where the murals were to be placed. Sadly, the quality of these murals, whatever their precise stylistic allegiance, is almost uniformly mediocre. Yet both the subject-matter and the different styles chosen tell us a good deal about what the American public expected from art. For example, the largest category, so far as the subject-matter itself was concerned, consists of costume pieces recording the moment when a particular community was founded. Clearly these fulfilled a psychological need, but they have nothing to do with avant-garde art – they occupy a stylistic backwater. Yet many other aspects of the murals are instructive and interesting.

Not surprisingly, for example, the commissions often led to sharp conflicts between the central authorities, as representatives of certain kinds of élite taste, and the people for whom the murals were designed. Yet local reaction was not always predictable. Lloyd Ney's mural *New London Facets* (1940), painted for the post office at New London, Ohio, is one of the most 'modernistic' thrown up by the entire programme, indeed it seems like a forerunner of Pop Art. It therefore comes as a surprise to discover that on this occasion the local community enthusiastically supported the artist against a reluctant central authority.

In commissioning these murals, the representatives of Federal government were always bedevilled by fears that the artists would introduce unacceptable political allusions. The PWAP had got off to a shaky start in 1934 when twenty-five artists were commissioned to decorate the Coit Tower in San Francisco, a newly completed memorial to the volunteer firemen of the city. Some proceeded to use

their paintings as a vehicle for the expression of left-wing opinions. Clifford Wight, an associate of Rivera, provided a sequence of three panels entitled respectively, *Rugged Individualism*, *The New Deal*, and *Communism*. His triptych left no doubt that the third alternative was the preferable one.

Another frequent subject of dispute was supposed sexual innuendo. On occasion, some of the painters were deliberately provocative. Paul Cadmus, commissioned in 1937 to produce a mural showing *Pocahontas Saving the Life of Captain John Smith* for the Parcel Post Building in Richmond, Virginia, introduced some suggestively posed Indian assailants, clad in very little. One virile figure had the head of a skinned fox dangling provocatively between his legs – it bore a marked resemblance to a penis. Cadmus, who revelled in this kind of joke, engaged in a long correspondence with the authorities, trying to get them to say what precisely it was that offended them.

151. Ad Reinhardt
Untitled, 1938

Oil on canvas
16 × 20in/40.6 × 50.8cm
The Museum of Modern Art, New York (Gift of the artist)

The patronage offered to artists by the Section of Fine Arts was very considerable, but it was dwarfed by the other assistance offered to artists by the government. In May 1935, almost a year after the cessation of the original PWAP, the Works Project Administration was established, under the overall charge of the Federal Emergency Relief Administrator, Harry Hopkins. This in turn spawned two relief programmes designed specifically to help artists. One was the Treasury Relief Art Project already referred to. The other – the WPA Federal Art Project (generally referred to simply as FPA) had a much further reaching effect. Until it was liquidated in 1943 it was responsible for the production not only of murals, but of sculptures, easel paintings, prints and posters, and for the establishment of community art centres and Federally sponsored art galleries. The FPA took two directions – towards the American public at large, and towards the art community. Unquestionably it promoted a much wider public awareness of art than America had known previously. But to the artists this, though important in itself, took second place to the mere fact that it enabled them to survive and continue to work. One artist, writing retrospectively in 1977, said:

> The WPA to me and all of the other artists on the Project in the '30s meant being able to continue in our profession. The $21 a week we received as wages was a gold mine. We painted hard and painted what we wanted to paint. Most of us accepted the depression and what it meant to America.

Another said:

> The years I worked on the WPA Art Project were the most meaningful and the happiest of my professional life. I felt a sense of purpose, a closeness to the people with whom we shared our economic plight, a feeling of being needed by them . . . There was a close comradeship among the artists . . . We were not degraded by personal opportunism, we were not manipulated by art entrepreneurs, critics nor museums . . . Together . . . we were creating a people's art.

252

Holger Cahill, the National Director of the FPA, made no formal distinction between abstract and figurative art. As a result major or soon to be major avant-garde artists like Gorky and Reinhardt were given opportunities to paint full-time which would previously not have been available to them. They also, as a result of being brought together on communal enterprises, developed an *esprit de corps* which was entirely novel in American art. Yet the conditions they were forced to endure were sometimes very hard: Arshile Gorky once said that it was impossible to live through the experiences of those years without being marked by them.

In trying to assess the effect of the FPA quite a large number of different factors have to be taken into account. One is the barren political factionalism it encouraged among certain artists, especially in the hot-house art-world of New York. Even artists whose work was not overtly political nevertheless felt compelled to organize politically. A case in point was Stuart Davis whose productivity, as we have already seen, fell because of the time and energy absorbed by other commitments, and who was finally embittered and disillusioned by the result. The political climate of the New York art-world was eventually to be affected by events outside America – the Moscow show trials and later the Hitler–Stalin pact. These were a shock for many idealistic artists and divided them from a remaining rump of Stalinist hardliners.

Another factor that must be taken into account when the FPA is assessed is the quality of the art itself. It reached levels higher than those reached by the post office murals, but it seldom represented the

152. Arshile Gorky
Study for a mural for the Administrative Building, Newark Airport, New Jersey, 1935–6

Gouache 13 × 29in/33 × 73.6cm
On extended loan to The Museum of Modern Art, New York, from the United States WPA Art Program

151
152 best work of the artists concerned. Reinhardt, Gorky and certainly Jackson Pollock will be remembered, not for what the FPA helped them to produce, but for what they did after the programme had ceased to exist.

In addition, it is perhaps significant that work made under FPA auspices seems to have had a rather low rate of physical survival. Gorky's mural for Newark airport, certainly one of his major achievements in the late 1930s, no longer exists, and the same is true of many other murals painted in similar circumstances at the same period. The FPA may have helped to open the ordinary citizen's eyes to the existence of Modernism, but it did not establish Modernism strongly enough to make sure than its own legacy of art-works was duly cherished.

In fact, what the FPA did was different in many ways from what its creators intended it to do. It kept artists alive, and it even gave the more avant-garde ones advantages they might not have enjoyed in a prosperous America where the success of an artist, and his ability to go on working, depended purely on the reactions of the market-place. Artists sensed that the work they were producing under the Project's auspices was directed at a new audience – the art community itself, not at the public at large. It was the first time that American artists had acquired a collective identity. The period saw, especially in New York, a ferment of discussion and experimentation, made possible quite largely by FPA subsidies. Hans Hofmann's teaching was beginning to have its effect; young artists like Jackson Pollock, who began his career as a pupil and follower of Benton, were struggling to find their own identities. The public art that the decade favoured concealed something very different that was taking place in private. It is this second development that seems to have major importance now, but the other, once-triumphant set of values should also be given its due – the concrete, visible achievements of American art during the decade were for the most part those of the realists, but the future belonged to artists who espoused a different cause.

Chronology

1930

Wilhelm Frick becomes the first Nazi minister holding office in the state of Thuringia.

Heinrich Brüning forms a right-wing coalition government in Germany.

Ras Tafari becomes the Emperor Haile Selassie of Ethiopia.

The last allied troops leave the Rhineland.

Catholic-Fascist Heimwehr units are set up in Austria under Prince Starhemberg.

Pilsudski forms a right-wing government in Poland.

There is a revolution in Argentina.

The Nazis win 107 seats in the German Reichstag, making gains from the centre parties.

There is a revolution in Brazil. Vargas becomes President.

1931

Pierre Laval becomes Prime Minister of France.

Oswald Mosley breaks with the British Labour Party in order to found the New Party along Fascist lines.

The Spanish Republic is proclaimed, and King Alfonso XIII goes into exile.

Collapse of the Austrian Credit-Anstalt creates a financial crisis throughout Central Europe.

Bankruptcy of German Danatbank leads to the closure of all German banks.

There is a British naval mutiny at Invergordon, due to pay cuts. A Heimwehr *coup d'état* fails in Austria.

Ramsay MacDonald forms the second National Government in Britain.

Sino-Japanese war. Japan withdraws from the League of Nations.

1932

The Indian Congress is declared illegal and Ghandi is arrested.

The Manchukuo Republic is proclaimed in Manchuria, following a Japanese invasion.

The Geneva Disarmament Conference takes place with no results. The Second Five-Year Plan begins in the USSR.

Eamonn de Valera is elected President of Eire.

Hindenburg defeats Hitler in the German Presidential election.

Franz von Papen becomes German Chancellor.

Salazar becomes Prime Minister of Portugal.

Roosevelt wins the US Presidency by a landslide.

Hitler receives German citizenship – previously not his because he was born in Austria.

Chaco War between Bolivia and Paraguay (to 1935).

1933

The United States grants independence to the Philippines.

Hitler becomes Chancellor of Germany; Germany leaves Geneva Disarmament Conference and League of Nations.

The Reichstag is destroyed in a fire.

Chancellor Dollfuss suspends parliamentary government in Austria.

Japan withdraws from the League of Nations.

Hitler is granted dictatorial powers.

The first concentration camps are set up in Germany.

Anti-Jewish laws are passed in Germany, and the German labour unions are suppressed.

The Public Works Administration is created in the United States.

The Nazi Party is suppressed in Austria.

All political parties, other than the Nazi party, are suppressed in Germany.

The United States recognizes the USSR and resumes trade.

Prohibition is repealed in America.

The Stavisky scandal breaks in France.

1934

Civil War in Austria – the socialists are suppressed.

There is a general strike in France.

Ghandi suspends his civil disobedience campaign in India.

Röhm and other Nazi opponents of Hitler are murdered.

Dolfuss, the Austrian Chancellor, is assassinated by the Nazis.

Hitler is appointed *Führer* in a German plebiscite.

The USSR is admitted to the League of Nations.

King Alexander of Yugoslavia and French Foreign Minister Paul Barthou are assassinated in Marseilles.

Purges begin in Russia after the assassination of Stalin's close collaborator Sergei Kirov.

China: 'Long March' north of Communist guerrillas under Mao Tse-tung.

1935

The Saarland is incorporated into Germany after a plebiscite.

The Nazis repudiate the treaty of Versailles and introduce conscription.

The Nuremberg laws are passed against the Jews.

The show trials begin in Russia.

King George V celebrates his Silver Jubilee in Britain.

Stanley Baldwin forms a National Government in Britain.

Italy invades Abyssinia; the League of Nations imposes trade sanctions.

Schusnigg, Dolfuss's successor, and Starhemberg stage an anti-Heimwehr *coup* in Austria.

Chiang Kai-shek is named President of the Chinese executive.

Tomás Masaryk resigns as President of Czechoslovakia and is succeeded by Edouard Beneš.

The Fascist Croix de Feu is formed in France.

1936

George V of England dies and is succeeded by his son Edward VIII.

German troops occupy the Rhineland.

Farouk becomes King of Egypt.

The Arab High Committee is formed to combat Jewish claims.

Italian troops occupy Addis Ababa and King Victor Emmanuel is proclaimed Emperor of Abyssinia.

General Francisco Franco rebels against the Spanish Republican Government and the Spanish Civil War begins.

Chiang Kai-shek enters Canton.

Mussolini and Hitler proclaim the Rome-Berlin Axis.

Roosevelt is re-elected President of the United States.

The Anti-Comintern pact is signed by Germany and Japan.

King Edward VIII abdicates to marry the American divorcee Mrs Simpson and is succeeded by his brother George VI.

Chiang Kai-shek declares war on Japan.

Trotsky is exiled from Russia and settles in Mexico.

Anglo-Egyptian Alliance is formed; British garrison in Suez Canal Zone.

1937

Poland refuses to sign an agreement to return Danzig to Germany.

There is a purge of Russian generals. Marshal Tukhachevsky is executed.

Guernica is destroyed by bombing; the Spanish Republican government moves to Barcelona.

All-India Congress Party wins elections.

Roosevelt signs the US Neutrality Act, guaranteeing American neutrality in the case of European war.

Baldwin retires and Neville Chamberlain becomes Prime Minister of Britain.

The Japanese seize Peking, Shanghai and Nanking; Chiang Kai-shek allies himself with the Communists, led by Mao-Tse-tung, and makes Chungking the capital of free China.

A Royal Commission on Palestine recommends the establishment of both Jewish and Arab states.

The Sudeten Germans leave the Czech Parliament, following riots in the Sudeten area of Czechoslovakia.

Italy joins the Anti-Comintern Pact.

Italy leaves the League of Nations.

Japanese planes attack and sink the US gunboat *Panay* in Chinese waters.

1938

The Japanese set up a Chinese puppet government in Nanking, and withdraw from the League of Nations.

Germany effects Anschluss with Austria.

The Sudeten Germans are denied autonomy by the Czechs; Germany mobilizes; Chamberlain visits Hitler at Berchesgarden and Godesberg; the Munich conference resulting in the Munich Agreement takes place in September, and Germany occupies the Sudetenland on 10 October.

Hungary annexes southern Slovakia.

In the USSR Bukharin and other old Bolsheviks are condemned in show trials.

Anti-Jewish laws are enacted in Italy.

1939

Germany occupies Bohemia and Moravia and places Slovakia under German 'protection', thus dismembering Czechoslovakia. Germany also renounces its non-aggression pact with Poland, concludes a ten-year alliance with Italy and a non-aggression pact with the USSR.

Britain and France recognize the Franco regime; Madrid falls and the Spanish Republican government collapses. Spain joins the Anti-Comintern Pact and leaves the League of Nations.

Italy invades Albania.

Hungary leaves the League of Nations.

Britain and Poland sign a treaty of mutual assistance.

Germany invades Poland and annexes Danzig (1 September); Britain and France declare war on Germany (3 September); Roosevelt declares the United States neutral; the USSR invades Poland from the East (17 September).

A British Expeditionary Force of 158,000 men is sent to France.

The USSR invades Finland (30 November) and is expelled from the League of Nations.

The German pocket battleship *Graf Spee* is sunk at the Battle of River Plate.

Bibliography

Dawn Ades, *Dalí*, London, Thames and Hudson, 1982; New York, Harper & Row

Sidney Alexander, *Marc Chagall*, London, Cassell, 1979

Gli Annitrenta – Catalogue of an exhibition held at the Palazzo Reale, Milan, and the Galleria del Sagrato, 27 January – 30 April 1972

The Avant-garde in Russia – catalogue of an exhibition held at the Los Angeles County Museum, 8 July–28 September 1980

Matthew Baigell, *Thomas Hart Benton*, New York, 1973

Alfred H. Barr, *Matisse: His Art and His Public*, New York, Museum of Modern Art, 1951

Stephanie Barron – *German Expressionist Sculpture* – Chicago and London, University of Chicago Press, 1983

Anthony Bertram, *Paul Nash: The Portrait of an Artist*, London, Faber, 1956

Bonnard: The Late Paintings – catalogue of an exhibition shown at the Musée National d'Art Moderne, Centre Georges Pompidou, Paris; The Phillips Collection, Washington D.C., and the Dallas Museum of Art, 1984

Arno Breker: *60 ans de sculpture*, Paris, 1981

ed. William Chappell, *Edward Burra: A Painter Remembered by His Friends*, London, André Deutsch with Lefevre Gallery, 1982

Wanda M. Corn, *Grant Wood: The Regionalist Vision*, New Haven and London, Yale University Press, 1983

Fleur Cowles, *The Case of Salvador Dalí*, London, Heinemann; Boston, Little Brown & Co, 1959

De Chirico – Catalogue of an exhibition held at the Museum of Modern Art, New York, and the Tate Gallery, London, 1982

Ian Dunlop, *The Shock of the New*, London, Weidenfeld and Nicolson, 1972; New York, American Heritage Press

Jacques Dupin, *Miró*, London, Thames and Hudson, 1962; New York, Harry N. Abrams

Emily Edwards, *Painted Walls of Mexico*, Austin and London, Texas University Press, 1966

Philip Eliasoph, *Paul Cadmus: Yesterday and Today*, Oxford, Ohio, Miami University Art Museum, 1981

Jacob Epstein, *Epstein, an autobiography*, 2nd ed. London, Vista Books, 1963; New York, Dutton Books

Justino Fernández, *A Guide to Mexican Art*, Chicago, London, University of Chicago Press, 1969

Friedhelm, W.Fischer, *Max Beckmann*, London, Phaidon Press, 1973

Laszlo Glozer, *westkunst: Zeitgenössische Kunst seit 1939*, Cologne, 1981

Ludwig Goldscheider, *Kokoschka*, London, Phaidon Press, 1963; Ontario, Burns & Mactarchen

Julio Gonzalez – Catalogue of an exhibition held at the Museum of Modern Art, New York, 1956

Otto Hahn – *André Masson* – London, Thames & Hudson; New York, 1965

George Heard Hamilton, *Painting and Sculpture in Europe 1880–1940*, 2nd ed. Harmondsworth, Middlesex, Penguin Books, 1971

A.M.Hammacher, *Barbara Hepworth*, London, Thames & Hudson, 1968; New York, Harry N.Abrams

Charles Harrison, *English Art and Modernism 1900–1939*, London, Penguin Books; Bloomington, Indiana, Indiana University Press, 1981

Nancy Heller and Julia Williams, *Painters of the American Scene*, 2nd ed. New York, 1982

Hayden Herrera, *Frida; a biography of Frida Kahlo*, London, New York, Harper & Row, 1983

Berthold Hinz, *Art in the Third Reich*, New York, Pantheon Books, 1980

BIBLIOGRAPHY

Robert Carleton Hobbs and Gail Levin, *Abstract Expressionism: The Formative Years*, Ithaca and London, Cornell University Press, 1978

Hommage à Elsa Schiaparelli – Catalogue of an exhibition held at the Musée de la Mode et du Costume, Palais Galliéra, Paris, 21 June–30 August 1984

P. Korma, *Pavel Korin*, Leningrad, 1972

ed. Richard Kostelanetz, *Moholy-Nagy*, London, Allen Lane, 1970; New York, Praeger Inc

ed. John R. Lane and Susan C. Larsen, *Abstract Painting and Sculpture in America*, Pittsburgh, Carnegie Institute Museum of Art, 1983

ed. A. Lebedev, *Soviet painting in the Tretyakov Gallery*, Leningrad, Aurora Art Publishers, 1976

Alain Lesieutre, *The Spirit and Splendour of Art Deco*, London, Paddington Press; New York, Two Continents Publishers, 1974

Gail Levin, *Edward Hopper: The Art and the Artist*, New York and London, W. W. Norton, with Whitney Museum of American Art, 1981.

Edward Lucie-Smith and Celestine Dars, *Work and Struggle*, London, Paddington Press; New York, 1977

Magish Realisme in Nederland – Catalogue of an exhibition held at the Museum of Fine Arts Antwerp, 18 September–14 November 1971

F. T. Marinetti, *Teria e invenzione Futurista*, Milan 1968

F. T. Marinetti, *Selected Writings*, edited and with an introduction by R. W. Flint, London, Secker & Warburg, 1972; New York, Farrar, Straus & Giroux

Karol Ann Marling, *Wall-to-Wall America*, Minneapolis, University of Minnesota Press, 1982

Carlos Merida, *Modern Mexican Artists*, 2nd ed. Freeport, New York, Books for Libraries Press, 1968

The James A. Michener Collection of Twentieth Century Painting, Austin, Texas, 1977

Richard Morphet, *Meredith Frampton*, London, Tate Gallery, 1982

Lynda Morris and Robert Radford – *The Story of the A.I.A.: Artists International Association, 1933–1953*, Oxford, 1983

Edwin Mullins, *Braque*, London, Thames and Hudson, 1968; New York, Harry N. Abrams

Maurice Nadeau, *The History of Surrealism*, London, Jonathan Cape; New York, Macmillan Inc, 1965

Neue Sachlichkeit and German Realism of the Twenties – Catalogue of an exhibition held at the Hayward Gallery, London, 11 November 1978 – 14 January 1979 Arts Council of Great Britain

Fritz Novotny, *Painting and sculpture in Europe 1780–1880*, 3rd ed. Harmondsworth, Middlesex, Penguin Books, 1978

Orozco – Catalogue of an exhibition held at the Museum of Modern Art, Oxford, 1980

Roy Oxlade, *David Bomberg, 1890–1957 (R.C.A. Papers No. 3)*, London, Royal College of Art, Kensington, 1977

Roland Penrose, *Picasso: His Life and Work*, London, Granada, 3rd edition, 1981

Picasso – Catalogue of an Exhibition held at the Tate Gallery, London, Arts Council of Great Britain, 6 July–18 September 1960

Picasso: *Sculpture, Ceramics and Graphic Work*, Catalogue of an exhibition held at the Tate Gallery, London, 9 June–13 August 1967

Picasso's Picassos – Catalogue of an exhibition held at the Hayward Gallery, London, Arts Council of Great Britain, 17 July–11 October 1981

Portuguese Art since 1910 – Catalogue of an exhibition held at the Royal Academy of Arts, London, 2 September–1 October 1978

Post-Impressionism: Cross-Currents in European Painting – Catalogue of an exhibition held at the Royal Academy of Arts, London, 1979–1980

Herbert Read, *Henry Moore*, London, Thames and Hudson, 1965; Collins/UNESCO

Les Réalismes 1919–1939 – Catalogue of an exhibition held at the Centre Georges Pompidou, Paris, 17 December – 20 April 1981

Hans K. Roethel, *Kandinsky*, London, Phaidon Press, 1979

Hans K. Roethel and Jean K. Benjamin – *Kandinsky, catalogue raisonné*, volume 2 – London, Sotheby Publishers, 1984

John Rothenstein, *Edward Burra*, London, Tate Gallery, 1973

John Russell, *Ben Nicholson*, London, Thames and Hudson, 1969

Russian and Soviet Painting – Catalogue of an exhibition held at the Metropolitan Museum of Art, New York, and the Fine Art Museums of San Francisco – New York, 1977

Uwe M. Schneede, *The Essential Max Ernst*, London, Thames and Hudson, 1973

Michel Seuphor, *Piet Mondrian: Life and work*, London, Thames and Hudson, 1957; New York, Harry N. Abrams

ed. David Shapiro, *Social Realism: Art as a Weapon*, New York, F. Ungar, 1973

Late Sickert; Painting 1927–1942 – Catalogue of an exhibition held at the Hayward Gallery, London, Arts Council of Great Britain, 18 November 1981–31 January 1982

James Thrall Soby, *Yves Tanguy*, New York, Museum of Modern Art, 1955

Natalya Sokolova, *Boris Ioganson*, Leningrad, 1982

Stanley Spencer R.A. – Catalogue of an exhibition held at the Royal Academy of Art, London, 20 September–14 December 1980

Werner Spies, *Josef Albers*, London, 1979

Denys Sutton, *André Derain*, London, Phaidon Press, 1959; New York, Doubleday

Raquel Tibol, *David Alfaro Siqueiros; un Mexicano y Su Obra*, Mexico City, 1969

Karen Tsujimoto, *Images of America: Precisionist Painting and Modern Photography*, Seattle and London, University of Washington Press, 1982

Sharyn Rohlfsen Udall, *Modernist Painting in New Mexico 1913–1935*, Albuquerque, University of New Mexico Press, 1984

William Vaughan, *German Romantic Painting*, Yale, Yale University Press, 1980

V. M. Volodarsky, *The Tretyakov Art Gallery: A Guide*, Moscow, 1977

Nicholas Watkins, *Matisse*, Oxford, Phaidon Press, 1984

John Willett, *The New Sobriety*, London, Thames and Hudson, 1978

Howard E. Wooden – *the Neglected Generation of American Realist Painters 1930–1948* – Catalogue of an exhibition held at the Wichita Art Museum, 3 May–14 June 1981

Vladislav Zimenko, *The Humanism of Art*, Moscow 1976

Index

The Reading Room Society
of St. Cloud

St. Cloud Public Library